I'd Rather Be A Mermaid

Mary Rebecca Lazier

ISBN 978-1-4357-0557-9

Cover by Mary Lazier and Mark Tichenor

Mary's pottery may be seen at *www.redhen.ca*

Published by Lulu.com

The author wishes to thank Ursula Crosbie, John Lazier, Carrole and Brian Blakeman for good suggestions and great encouragement. Susan MacDonald helped ferret out stubborn grammatical misdemeanors.

Hearty thanks to Mark Tichenor, my husband and computer wizard, without whose help I would still be scratching on the wall of my cave.

"It's a goddam embarrassment, publishing," he once said to a fellow writer. "The poor boob who lets himself in for it might as well walk down Madison Avenue with his pants down."

Margaret A. Salinger in her memoir, <u>Dream Catcher</u>,
quoting her father J.D. Salinger

And even if only one good memory is left in our hearts, it may also be the instrument of our salvation one day.

Fyodor Dostoyevsky
Brother Karamazov

Contents

Chapter One
My Father's Mustache

Our family name "Lazier" derives from the French Huguenot LeSueur family, who left France in the seventeenth century to find freedom from religious persecution. The Huguenots protested the rituals and the wealth of the Catholic Church and their Protestant religion was declared unlawful by Louis XIV. During the 16th Century in England, King Henry VIII left the Catholic Church and became Protestant because he wanted to divorce his first wife Katherine of Aragon to marry Anne Boleyn.

Francois LeSueur arrived in New Amsterdam, Long Island, April 10 1657 aboard "The Brindled Cow". One hundred and thirty-four years later, the family had a lot of land and a milling business in New York State, but when required to sign a statement of allegiance to the American government, they refused; their land was confiscated and they moved to Canada in 1791 with 9 children. They settled in Prince Edward County, Ontario. LaSueur gradually changed to Lazier. It is pronounced with the emphasis on the second syllable, rhyming with brassiere, except that the z sound is more zh. We don't pronounce it lazier like lying down, although there was once a law firm called

1

Lazier, Lazier and Doolittle. In high school, my brother John was called Bra, sister Annie was Brazier, and I was Mary Maidenform. Our motto was "Never fear! Lazier is here!"

The railways were built across the North American continent in the 1800s as part of the American "Manifest Destiny" policy to populate the west by offering free land to those who would farm it. The advertising was brilliant, newspapers and full colour booklets exhorted people to go west for the sunny skies of California, the rich soil of the prairies and certain financial success. The romance of the train promised to deliver you to paradise, and anyone who didn't want to go was thought to be crazy. "Go West Young Man Go West" was the rallying cry of the time.

Richard Lazier, second from lower left
Arthur Lazier top left

In 1901, the year that Queen Victoria died, great grandfather Richard and his wife went west to join their eldest son John, who had settled in Gonzales California in 1888. Gonzales was in the fertile Salinas Valley where crops grew all year long under sunny skies, and winter meant a dry spell, not five months of fierce Canadian blizzards.

Our grandfather, Arthur Lazier, was the youngest of Richard's children, and at twenty-two years of age, he went to work as a bookkeeper for his sister Anna, in Gladstone, Manitoba, where they had a printing business.

In 1901 the McClory family was farming near Gladstone, and their eldest daughter was to be our grandmother, Nellie McClory. Nellie and Arthur were neighbours, and as they were romantically inclined, they conceived our father before they were married. In a time when it was shocking to see a woman's ankle, Nellie's

Nellie ~ 1910

family was horrified at the shame she brought to the family, and the bad example she set for her two younger sisters. Some women of the time killed themselves trying to abort a baby; they used knitting needles, kerosene, mustard, and some drank poison. She has almost forty descendants who are glad she chose to marry and get out of town before anyone noticed that she was pregnant. They fled to Gonzales because Arthur knew he could work for his family.

3

The overland trip in winter was cold and uncomfortable. It was dangerous, with the western Indians upset by the loss of their lands, and it was bumpy in the horse-drawn coaches that joined up with the railway lines. There were freezing waits between trains and coaches. It must have been such a huge relief to arrive in sunny California!

Our father Morley, named for his maternal grandmother's maiden name, was born July 25 1903 in Gonzales. The family stayed until 1910 and then moved back to Manitoba where Arthur worked for his sister's business again. Morley was a difficult kid, he was disobedient, he had a penchant for crazy practical jokes, and he was obviously smarter than everyone else and he let them know it. He was

a prodigy in school, and in grade twelve, he built a large contraption with a glass box on top, which he rolled into his science class. He used hydrochloric acid for the hydrogen, and an electric spark came off an electrode. His teacher was amazed to see that this sixteen-year-old kid had figured out how to make water by combining gas and electricity. Chlorine gas came off as well; they had to open windows so they didn't all choke to death.

As a young man, he looked fabulous, a sort of urbane swashbuckler, with a personality made up of dollops of Erroll Flynn's handsome charm, Dorothy Parker's acid wit, and Richard Feynman's wonderful ability to impart the fun of physics. He had piercing blue eyes which bugged out a bit if you told him something interesting; then he would say, "Tell me more, you interest me strangely." He had a long upper lip, perfect for a mustache; he often wore a big silk bow tie and a fedora. After high school in 1920, he went to automobile school in Chicago, and then got a job at the car company Duesenberg in Indiana for a few years, to earn enough money for University. He studied Mechanical Engineering at University of Toronto. His friends at U. of T. included Bev Shenstone, another serious (male) engineering student, who wrote,

> *"He was by far the most brilliant man of his year, he was a little older than most of us: he had had jobs, he had been around, he had listened and absorbed. He was so quick to grasp problems, so clear in his thought, so sharp in his expression of them that he left us standing. He had the gift of intuitive understanding...we could not make the mental jumps he could and did make".*

Mental jumps were the only ones he did make. Later in his life, at dinnertime, he pounded his fist on the dining room table, making everything jump, and loudly declaimed,

> *"I have **never** to my knowledge committed an athletic act!"*

In 1928, Morley came after Lester B. Pearson as winner of the Massey Scholarship. Pop went to King's College, in Cambridge England, where he investigated fuel atomization in diesel engines. His professor stole his original material and published it with no reference to his name, so he left in a state of high indignation. The fact that he was not awarded a postgraduate degree annoyed him his entire life.

Cambridge in the late twenties was rife with Communist spies. Anthony Blunt, an aristocratic don at Trinity College Cambridge, was recruiting Communist sympathizers. The most famous among them were Kim Philby, Guy Burgess and Donald McLean. Even though most of them were at Trinity College studying Political Science, Fascists, Communists and intellectual iconoclasts were fomenting discontent everywhere. Besides that, Cambridge was an ancient seat of wisdom with incredible stone architecture, wonderful libraries and famous professors for the intellectual elite. England was delightfully bizarre, combining the aristocratic High Table with the Communist spies, and Pop could be as eccentric as he wanted. What a tremendous let down to come back to the turgid puritanical backwater that was Toronto in 1929.

Helen Gourley ~ 1930

Our mother was Helen Gourley, born in 1904 in Souris Manitoba. When Mum's Grandmother Susannah Bray died in Winnipeg in 1945, the obituary in The Winnipeg Free Press said that she had "settled at the end of steel", which was then Wolseley Saskatchewan. Mum's parents, Robert Gourley and Laura Bray met and married there. Both their families had gone west from Ontario.

Helen went to England, having graduated from the University of Manitoba. She had studied painting and printmaking with Walter J. Phillips, and in England she went to The Slade School of Fine Art. When she left Canada, she was engaged to be married to George Ferguson, who became the Editor of the Montreal Star, but when Helen met Morley, she changed her mind. Her traveling companion, Mary Doupe, went back to Winnipeg to tell George the bad news, and then married him herself.

Laura Gourley, centre, back row

Mum was the culture vulture, always dragging Morley off to cultural events. One time they went to the Tate Gallery in London to see a show. Pop was up close, examining the brush-strokes on a painting, when he noticed someone glide up to inspect the same painting. It was Queen Mary herself, a very imposing personage. She was tall and straight, magnificently dressed, and always wore ropes of wonderful pearls. He didn't have any idea what the protocol was for meeting the Queen, so, amazed at himself for having nothing smart to say, he scuttled off backwards like a crab, bumped into Mum as he escaped, and said, "Yeah!" Another time they went to a concert in a hall with hard seats. Pop always had wooden matches in his back pocket for lighting his cigarettes, and when he shifted around in the seat, they caught fire. With his pants ablaze, he stepped in front of the people in his row, "Excuse me madam (or sir), I'm on fire" he said to each person as he stepped in front of them. He raced off up the aisle and sat in a drinking fountain. He finished the concert in a very uncomfortable pair of pants. His discomfort probably extended to the fact that he was cooped up in an auditorium. Pop preferred to experiment with things while he listened to Fats Waller playing on the radio. "Fetch me my Gin, son 'fore I tan your hide" and "Who's dat walking around up dere - sounds like baby elephant pattah. You your big feets and me" were his favourite lines. He could imitate Fats very well and even looked quite like him, with a cigarette dangling from his lip.

Our parents were married in Winnipeg, September 1930. Pop had a job teaching engineering students at the University of Toronto. His students remember that he would spend half a day creating an enormous coloured chalk drawing of an engine just to demonstrate a spark plug, and that he could talk forever on any subject. He took a serious approach to the great questions of the universe, one of his favourites was "When is now?" He had an ability to teach people to think rather than to memorize, and in an amusing way, he was able to impart his great curiosity and love of discovery.

Remembering the glorious days of Cambridge and "High Table", he arranged huge dinners in Hart House on the University of Toronto campus for professors and students, when the whole dining room was lit by hundreds of candles. Hart House was a beautiful old

8

stone building by Canadian standards, but a few hundred years younger than the Cambridge campus.

For a few years he enjoyed teaching, learning about aircraft design from Tommy R. Louden, his mentor, and impressing a coterie of brilliant students. When the second world war became a Canadian concern, Massey Harris seconded him to their plant, which had been converted from farm machinery to building parts for the Mosquito, a bomber made of balsa wood. The Mosquito was so light that it could fly at thirty thousand feet to do reconnaissance and take pictures of installations in enemy territory for the follow-up Lancaster bombers. Pop was a manager in the plant, but bossing people around was not his idea of fun. Even though he didn't have to go to war, he was seriously stressed by the long hours and huge responsibility of it, and he started to drink too much. He was lonely too. He didn't have enough friends who spoke his language, his wife shunned him because he was about as domesticated as a mountain goat, squalling children came along to interrupt his sleep and he took comfort in increasingly larger amounts of gin. He came home very late at night, usually drunk and outraged at his inability to appease the furies that pursued him. He roared and raged and threatened anyone in his path. I hid in bed, stuffed pillows in my ears and hummed until I went back to sleep.

When Annie was born in 1934, Mum tried to get Morley to hold her. He flinched, and said, "Ugh! It looks so *human!*" He wasn't the least bit interested in becoming a father, and he thought babies and young children were quite repulsive.

Our mother wasn't exactly warm and fuzzy, but she was intent on bringing us up to be proper ladies and gentlemen. She wanted us to reflect well on her. Annie and I had hats and gloves for special occasions; we always wore dresses or skirts. Jeans were only worn by farmers, and so repressed was life in North Toronto that John was sent home from high school for wearing Bermuda shorts with knee socks. He thought he was the height of new fashion, but the school thought that knees were somehow obscene.

In 1937 Pop wrote of his discontent to his friend Bev. Shenstone:

> *"It may be that I might even acquire the ability to express myself in writing, and give up the keeping of hours and hungering after a millennial workshop where everybody makes things they like for people who want them. Meanwhile walk peacefully and stuff your ears with inattention when women's minds annoy you, as all men in the world have done, and will do without end."*

The part about the workshop amazes me now because our pottery studio is a place where happy people make things for people who want them. He would have said our workshop was a "dilly thing" because it's fun and it works. Dilly in the Thesaurus is a synonym with peach, ace, and the cat's pajamas. To him, making things and experimenting with gravity were much more interesting than having to work for somebody else for a salary. He invented diesel-fuelling, wallboard made out of sawdust and glue, and a method of taking the ink out of newspaper for recycling. It's too bad that he never patented any of his inventions; he was ahead of his time from his very conception, but his creative genius needed a dollop of Henry Ford or Bill Gates' business acumen. He should have followed his own advice to "be as persistent as a boil on yer ass", because he always gave up too easily.

Gourley grandparents ~ 1945

My first memory is of my maternal grandmother coming to Toronto for a visit. She was tall, with elegant posture, la belle poitrine and impressive pearls. She was austere and regal like Queen Mary Herself.

Grandmother had been visiting her youngest daughter Beth in Montreal who was working in Wilder Penfield's lab at the Neurological Institute. Incidentally, she also made bathtub gin for Morley. Grandmother had been hospitalized in Montreal with a recurrence of chronic bronchial asthma, and she died of it soon after she returned to Winnipeg. Her death meant that our aunt Gracie had to leave our household and her job as a nurse-Xray technician at The Toronto General Hospital. She was my absolutely favourite person because she always had time for me, and she knew about unconditional love. I filled a space for her too, because she never married and didn't have children. I spent a lot of time with Gracie when she lived with us, and when John broke his arm in 1946, it was such a bad break that he had to stay in hospital for a few days. Gracie and I went to see him, and as we walked down the hospital corridor, I saw one of those big brass fire extinguishers with a hose coming out the side. I asked her what it was, and looking further down the hall, she said, "Oh that's an iron lung, they put people in there when they have polio, it helps them breathe." We were warned about polio constantly; no public swimming pools, no movies, no going to the fall fair. Stay away from large groups of people, don't sit in a wet bathing suit ... on and on it went. Clouds of polio germs were lurking everywhere. After thinking about being squeezed into that fire extinguisher, I was well and truly warned. That summer I had my tonsils out on the kitchen table at home. The hospitals were full of men returning from the war, and our doctor, who was named Dr. Perfect, said it would be easier and faster to do it at home. He used my washcloth to administer the ether, and he lied when he said it would smell like a banana split He didn't do a great job because he had to do it again 5 years later.

I went to live with Gracie and Grandfather in Winnipeg for the winter after Grandmother Gourley died. It was a relief for her to move back to Winnipeg, because at our house, Pop had the habit of going into her room late at night, turning Grandfather's picture to the wall and then screaming at her in a drunken rage. Sometimes Mum and Annie would go down in the middle of the night and they would all scream at each other.

Living with Gracie in Winnipeg was wonderful because she wasn't neurotic, she was so patient and peaceful, she liked to make things, and she treated me like the favourite pet of the household. It didn't last long though, because I had to start school in Toronto.

I was "The Lost Child" in our dysfunctional family, Annie was "The Scapegoat" and John was "The Hero", all roles defined by books about children of alcoholics. At dinnertime I felt like the only member of Densa at a Mensa meeting of brilliant people because I could never be as smart or witty as they were. Annie once said, "You will never be as smart as me!" and I retorted, "Not till you're dead!"

I was always at the bottom of the heap, terrified of the forceful personalities surrounding me, and fearful of a father who was often a raving drunk. This was before the time of therapy for children of alcoholics, co-dependents, or even acknowledgment.

Our house on Glengrove sat on the northern edge of Toronto, which was south of Lawrence Avenue. Across the street from us there were fields, streams, bunnies and birds. Thousands of houses were built to the north of us during the forties. Our milkman came from Uplands Dairy, and his cart was pulled by an ornery horse. More than once that horse jumped up over the curb and chased us. The local boys played road hockey with the conveniently round horse droppings called road apples. Forty five years later, I told this story to my eight year old grand-daughter Mia, and the following week, she said, "Tell me again how the boys played hockey with frozen cow pies", and her mother Sara said, without skipping a beat, "Oh no, that's how the Canadians invented Curling!"

Coal for the furnace was delivered in a truck, and it was poured down a chute into the basement through a window. The deliverymen were blacker than Africans from the coal dust – their lungs too. The coal had to be picked up in a shovel and heaved into the furnace several times a day, and the cinders or "clinkers" had to be shoveled out of the bottom of the furnace into huge metal bins. In grade eight, I ran for mayor of my school, John Ross Robertson Public School, and my major platform was that I would replace the cinders spread over the playground with grass. The other kids at school laughed at me as though I was some kind of crazy nut, and that was impossible. They didn't elect me, but there's grass growing there now.

Old Man Morrow was our neighbour across the street, he dressed like a scarecrow and he was built like one too. He was pale, and so bony that he seemed to be constructed of sticks. Pop had his Chow dog put down after it bit Annie and him, so there was a complete lack of neighbourliness there. John and his friends played hockey and football on the street and it drove Morrow crazy. He was always phoning the cops because the football hit the phone wires. One long May weekend I went to a friend's cottage and when we got home, Morrow was chasing a bunch of kids down the street with a gun. They had blown up all his big tulips with ladyfinger firecrackers.

In the long June evenings the kids on the block played Kick the Can, and sometimes Mrs. A. would come by. She was the mother of one of John's friends, and she careened around on a bicycle in big wobbly loops because she was always so drunk. She dressed in a glamorous way with long flowing dresses and scarves. Her face had been beautiful, but so lined with sadness that it seemed that she didn't get it on quite straight in the morning. Her lipstick was off center, mascara was all over her cheeks, and her beautiful wavy hair was full of hairpins sticking out in all directions, not doing much of a job of keeping it up. She was obviously desperately lonely, and the kids used to enjoy talking to her because she was such a character, and she actually seemed to like us. One night she sang a slow version of "Lili Marlene" and did a strip tease right down to the buff under the streetlight. We were about twelve years old. I had never seen a naked person before, so it was an amazing evening. Our parents never knew what we did out there on the street, in retrospect it wasn't so bad, but that could never happen now.

Mary Lynn Gibbons was my best friend on the street. I shortened her name to Gibbies because Marys was confusing. I think we spent most of our lives outside, skipping, roller skating, playing Ungi Mungi with rubber balls against the wall, a game of hopping over an elastic called "Yoki in the Kaiser", marbles, jacks, and kick-the-can. All the girls babysat for extra money. We earned twenty-five cents an hour, and when I worked all summer as a mother's helper, I

14

was paid ten dollars a week. One family I worked for had a nasty bull dog named Sally, who clamped onto my arm one evening when I answered the phone in their kitchen. The dog wouldn't let go, so I phoned home for help, but none was forthcoming. I finally got her to let go when I found some dog treats on the counter.

Our next-door neighbour was a well-known judge who sent two of the famous Boyd Gang to the gallows. They were a wildly brazen gang of bank robbers, and it was thrilling to read about them in our evening newspaper, "The Pink Telly". In fact they were folk heroes, the newspapers were full of photographs and stories of their exploits. Edwin Alonzo Boyd escaped from the Toronto Don Jail and with three pals went on a bank-robbing spree, Steve Suchan, one of the gang members, hid out at his father's house. The father persuaded the gang to hide the money under the floorboards, and the next day he went to Florida for three months. He spent all the money, so the gang had to rob another bank. Apparently while in hiding, Boyd dressed as a woman so he could go out on the town. In March they robbed the Leaside branch of the Bank of Montreal of $24,000, which was the biggest robbery in the history of Toronto. Finally two members of the gang were confronted by two policemen, and one of the policemen died in the shoot-out. Steve Suchan and Lennie Jackson were hung back to back, and Boyd went to the Kingston penitentiary for ten years.

The judge was a friend of Igor Gouzenko, a Russian spy who defected to Canada in the fifties. He was important because he exposed Russia's attempt to steal secrets from Canada and the United States. Until then, Russia and Canada had been allies. Whenever he was on TV or in the papers, he had his head in a large cloth bag, which came down to his shoulders, so he couldn't be recognized and captured by

Igor Gouzenko

the KGB. I thought he wore the bag all the time, but even though I watched and waited, I never saw a man with a bag on his head get out of a car to visit the judge.

Going back to school on Labour Day was the best day of the year, because I could get away from home for hours at a time. Standing at the top of my class made me feel smart, and I often had teachers who had dealt with Annie. They ordered, "Sit at the front! I have to keep an eye on you!" I learned to hold a quill pen correctly so it didn't splat on the page, I was good at arithmetic and social studies, but we had the dumbest books for reading. *See Spot Run, Oh, Oh, see him run. "There is Puff," said Jane.* We also learned to be seen and not heard, so there was no complaining allowed about the idiotic stuff we had to read.

I went to school early to play with friends, and I stayed late for special art classes. The art classes are embarrassing to remember. We glued shells together into ugly bunches and gave them as broaches to our mothers. We also made plaster molds of little ladies in dresses and painted them. Our poor mothers, what an amazing pile of dreck they had at the end of the year. I won a few prizes for paintings, but Annie was taking her art very seriously by then, and she didn't like competition. Once she looked at one of my paintings, and snorted "Trees aren't brown, they're grey!" Later on, she painted trees that were purple, but I learned early never to argue with Annie, never to make her wrong, never to confront her. It was safer for me to hide in my room when I was in the house. In there I read, made little things and folded Origami paper. I never had clay to work with, but I had a great battery operated nail-filing kit, somewhat like a Kiddy Dremel.

(Trying it on fingernails would have eliminated them). It was great for shaping and sanding bits of balsa wood, and cleaning off glue. I was famous as a kid for my amazing sore throats, and for relief I took something called "Elixir of Turpin Hydrate", a delicious concoction of alcohol and codeine. It tasted like Quantro, and it made me feel wonderful. Years later I was told that it wasn't available by prescription anymore. The Doctor was shocked that I even knew about it.

When I was about twelve, Mum took us to Buffalo for Easter weekend. She was looking for a brand of girl's clothing called "Chubettes" because she couldn't find any clothes to fit me in Canada: not very flattering at all. Chubettes were too big for me, but my lifelong sensitivity about "looking fat" stems from that expedition. Since then, I have been on every conceivable diet, and about 800 pounds have been gained and lost in a variety of ways.

Annie was the Scapegoat in the family, she skipped school and went to the movies, she was irreverent towards our parents, she never conformed to the rules of school, exams, or respect for our elders. There was a reform school not far from our house; it was a huge gray stone edifice with bars on the windows. Every time we passed it on a Sunday drive, our parents would say, "See that reform school Annie? One more problem from you, and that's where you're going". I was as good as she was bad, terrified of authority, I never asked questions in public, and never put my hand up because I was learning to be invisible.

For Halloween 1952, Mum made me a costume to go out as Alice in Wonderland. It had striped socks, a white pinnie and a lovely wig made out of yellow wool. She was a member of The Home and School Association, and very keen on the school's Halloween party because it kept the kids off the streets. As well as making my costume, she made big cutout signs for the school party. She had spent weeks getting ready for the big night, and as we were leaving the house, Pop was standing next to the fireplace with a tiny glass in his hand.

"Don't drink too much" she admonished him.

"Oh no, angel, I just have this tiny glass" he replied.

We had a great evening at the school with costume competitions, a parade, and performances in the auditorium by each class and hot dogs before we went home. Mum stayed to clean up, and I walked home with my friends, "shelling out" on the way. Across the street from our house, I saw our front door open, a brilliant floodlight came on suddenly, and a short little monster in a long black cloak was chasing some children who were running away screaming. Pop had lots of time that evening to find kneepads, the cloak, and the over-sized hideous hairy mask made by his friend Merle Foster. He set the lights up in the front hall so he could turn them on himself as he opened the door, which scared the bejesus out of the kids. I didn't go home until I saw Mum's car in the driveway.

Chapter Two
A Rain of Frogs

My family terrified me, and in self-defense, I learned to avoid confrontation, being questioned, and having to make up lies on the spot. Annie was mean because she didn't think I should even have existed, so I survived by hiding. I made myself invisible. In the summers I spent a lot of time underground in forts, which my neighbourhood friend Chris and I dug in the field across the street. Maybe it was a remnant of the war, pretending that it was a real dug - out, or maybe we both needed to escape. We dug a big hole, covered it over with boards and sod, took sufficient amounts of food and Freshie, our hoard of comic books, and spend hours underground, reading by flashlights.

For weeks one summer I slept in a refrigerator box in a neighbour's backyard. This family was very nice to me because the father of the family was an engineer and he had been a student of Pop's. They didn't talk to each other particularly, but Mr. Morse had a sort of reverence for Mr. Lazier that worked to my advantage. I was always welcome there, and I loved the family. They were nice to each other and didn't bicker all the time. They all worried about the fact that I was a little heathen, though. My friend Marilyn was the only daughter in the family and she was especially concerned, because she was getting fresh daily doses of catechism at her Catholic School. She said that she would pray for me, and she could get nuns to pray for me too, but no matter how hard she tried, she could never get me out of Limbo if I didn't get baptized.

I practically lived at their house on the weekends, we slept in Marilyn's frilly room, and for entertainment, we made fudge and moved the furniture around in her room. For some reason it was against the rules to move the furniture every Friday night, so we had to lift everything so the family downstairs wouldn't hear. There was hell to pay on Saturday, but there was always the challenge to do it without anyone knowing.

Marilyn persuaded me that I had to get baptized and confirmed, but she was nice enough to allow me to be a Protestant, like my Huguenot ancestors. I did, but then the Pope eliminated Limbo.

Hiding at their house on the weekend was eliminated one Friday when Marilyn said "Did I ask you to come over here?" and it was all over for me at their house. I had to amuse myself at home, where I hid in my room, making little things and reading books.

When I was fourteen, we were having a big Sunday dinner with some guests, when Mum asked me if I believed in "premarital interdigitation". Luckily I knew what a digit was, and could figure out that she meant holding hands, but she only asked me that as a challenge, it wasn't gentle guidance. She loved words and their derivations. Once she was creeping up on the pressure cooker with a long kitchen fork in her outstretched arm. She was going to flip the little top off to let some steam out. Just at that moment I told her that my friend Janet was such a brown-noser. She stopped, gave me the 100 watt glare that singed my eyebrows and said; "Did you ever think about what that *means*?"

Another time she tore a strip off my friend Peter when he used the word "irregardless". Didn't he know that was a double negative? Did he mean to say "regardless" or "irrespective"?

Our Mother was very intelligent, well educated, and the eldest in her family of five children. She said that her father had to buy The Encyclopedia Britannica when she left home. Jobs were for men so she never had one. After the wars, the men coming back had to have work, and women were not expected to have to support their families. She painted landscapes in oil quite well, but never sold anything that I know of. Modesty was carefully cultivated in our household, and perhaps selling her work would have been immodest. She enjoyed painting on weekends in the country around Toronto, and at the Lake of the Woods.

She was a charter member of her sorority in Winnipeg, and as early feminists they protested not having the vote by not wearing underpants for an unspecified length of time in the 20s. But who knew?

It seems to me that as a married woman she must have rebelled against spending all of her time doing housework, because when she was growing up in Winnipeg, they had a housekeeper and a maid. The only domestic thing I ever heard from her about her youth was that as a youngster she had to go to the basement to get eggs, which were stored in a big barrel full of sodium silicate. She had to stick her arm into this cold slimy liquid to get the eggs, which were preserved that way before electric refrigerators. Grandmother Gourley didn't have to spend her time shopping, cooking and doing laundry because she was wealthy and she had three or four employees to do the household work.

Grandfather Gourley left his family at a young age, he achieved a grade eight certificate, and then went to work. He had an entrepreneurial spirit, but he found that delivering water to the men who built the railway earned him only ten cents a day, so he went to work for the Union Bank where he followed Gilbert and Sullivan's advice in "Pinafore". He "cleaned the windows and he swept the floor, and he polished up the handle of the big front door. He polished up that handle so carefully, that now he is the ruler of the Queen's Navy." Before he was 21 he was a manager in the bank, and had bought and sold a lumber company with a profit of $20,000, which was a fortune in those days. By the time he was thirty, he was a part owner of The Beaver Lumber Company, and he was making money and becoming a big player in the west. His advice about success in business was,

> "All he has to do is get his foot in the door and make himself indispensable. First at the office in the morning. Last to go. Find something to do which someone else would do if he hadn't done it first. Cater to the seniors. There is no easy way in this world, and nothing is more satisfying than work."

Mum was not prepared for the grind of running a house by herself. We had an electric washing machine, but it only washed, everything had to be put through the wringer into big tubs for rinsing and then hauled upstairs to be hung on the clothesline where it froze solid during the winter. Getting the laundry on the line before anyone else on Mondays was a competition with the alpha females. The neighbours were also concerned about what went on the line. I heard a story about a woman who was given a pair of men's pajamas to hang out every week because the local ladies were scandalized by the fact that the man of the house didn't wear pajamas, and they knew because none went on the line on Monday.

On Tuesdays, Mum ironed the sheets in a "mangle". Then all the shirts and dresses for a family of five, she must have felt like one of her mother's maids. One day when I was about 9, she was ironing sheets as I came home from school and from the door way I accused her:

"You told me babies came from storks."

"I did not!" she shot back.

"Where do they come from then?" I asked.

"They come from eggs." Case dismissed.

This was a curious thing. Eggs, like the ones in the refrigerator? Why had nobody mentioned this before?

Information about our bodies was not readily available, but we found magazines in the house, which had a few clues. One was "Ladies Home Journal" which had a column called *Tell Me Doctor*. John got it out of the garbage, and I snuck it out of his room and put it back in the garbage after reading the juicy bits.

Our house had a great basement room with a fireplace and big west-facing windows, but Pop turned it into his evil smelling workshop. It was the men's room, no kids allowed. I was invited down only once, March 31 1951, because he wanted me to help him with an April Fool's project. I had to surreptitiously collect all the bars of soap in the house and take them downstairs where we varnished them.

23

When they were dry I put them back at each sink and bathtub. We thought this was the funniest thing in the world the next day when people were having showers.

In his workshop he had big tools; lathe, drill press, table saw, drafting table, an oscilloscope, lots of oily old engines and a big mess of small tools. There were wooden racks on the walls to hold metal "flat fifty" cigarette boxes in which he kept nuts and bolts, screws, tiny springs, and small stuff. All the work surfaces were decorated with parallel cigarette burns. The smell was vile; methyl-ethyl-ketone, solvents, sawdust, his favourite glue, Pliobond, oil from the engines, and pails full of sand and dead cigarettes. It's a wonder it didn't spontaneously ignite with the fumes and the cigarettes.

Pop built a lot of furniture when they first moved in in 1940; an 8-foot bookcase, a bed with 2 bedside cupboards. Later on, a doll's house for Annie and a baby jail for me. The baby jail was a Christmas request, and he made it out of a butter box with tiny windows with bars and a door on hinges. I had intended to keep bad dolls in there, but usually it was the family cat. John had the same inventive mind as Pop. He made a remote controlled car that ran over his bed. When he had German Measles he entertained himself running the car back and forth on string tracks over his bed.

Strange men who were known by Pop worked downstairs in the basement doing mysterious things. One project was to make DINK (which stood for De Ink); they used it to remove ink from newspaper to make it recyclable. The newspaper was mushed up in the laundry sink and mixed with detergents to clean it. The result was a gray pulp, not very useful.

With Bill Sheldon, Pop made wallboard out of pressed sawdust and glue. Very pleased with themselves, they brought a piece of it to the dinner table.

"Look Morley! I can stick my finger through it!" said Jeanie Sheldon.

"Well don't!!" said the men. In both cases he was ahead of his time and he could have been more persistent.

In 1948, they were looking for oil using radio waves. For this they used one car full of radio equipment to send a signal. Another car drove around the back roads receiving the signal on a chart recorder. The signal traveling through the earth pinpointed some promising spots, but they never found oil in commercial quantities.

Even though he scared me half to death, when I was in grade three, Pop taught me how to use a slide rule so I wouldn't waste my brainpower on learning the multiplication tables. I went to him when I was nine and said, "I saw eight robins in the back yard this morning".

"Tell me more, you interest me strangely. Did they have names?"

"No, they didn't" I replied.

"Did they have numbers on them?' he persisted.

"You think I saw the same robin eight times, don't you?" as the light bulb went on in my head.

The longest conversation I remember having with him was after dinner one night in 1951. He was lying on the living room floor on his back with his knees up. "Hey Shrimpo," he said, "come on over here and tell me everything you know about witches!"

Luckily, this was a subject I was prepared to discuss. I was thrilled to tell him the story of Baba Yaga, the famous Russian witch who rode around the forest in a mortar and pestle. She had iron teeth and ate little girls for breakfast. In her house, which perched on chicken legs, she kept a skinny black cat that had previously been Prince Ivan. It was a great long tale, and he was spellbound. I had finally made an impression on him!

He was fond of Merle Foster, a woman he had met at De Havilland, and he wrote to Walt Kelly asking him to include her name in one of his comic strips. She appeared on the back of the punt carrying Pogo and Albert as the name of the boat "The Good Ole Merle Foster". I was never convinced that Pop traded in his chilly wife for the warm and cozy Miss Foster, but Annie claimed that he was in his undershorts one Saturday morning at Merle's house when Annie and her boyfriend had gone to collect the rent. (The boyfriend's father owned Merles's house)

Pop left home in 1952, he said he hadn't had a holiday for a long time, and he was going to California. I think everyone else in the household knew that he was leaving for good, but I had to figure it out by myself. "Little pitchers have big ears" abbreviated to "'Lil pitchers" was the code word for everyone to stop talking when I came into the room. Pop was in bad shape when he left, and relief was my most memorable emotion. At last I could bring my friends home and get a full night's sleep without him ranting and threatening Mum and Annie all night long.

He took the bus, but ended up in a mental hospital in Sacramento because he was found on the street with the DTs. During the 90 days he spent there, he rebuilt all of their sewing machines, redesigned the hospital gowns and made new ones out of sheets. He disliked that breeze in the back of the regular gowns with one little tie at the back of the neck.

We had a modest little piano in the living room; our parents bought it from a de-commissioned destroyer after the war. This was before television, and there were many joyful evenings singing around the piano with our family friend Dickie Blue playing from the Oxford Song Book. Mum didn't play with as much assurance and enthusiasm as Dickie Blue, but we sat for hours when I was young, singing English ballads.

Eventually I started to study the piano with Miss Betty Wright, who adhered strictly to the Conservatory of Music curriculum. She was small and mean; she had big tombstone teeth and an enormous goiter, which matched tiny arthritic goiters she had on each finger joint. Her hair was wound around her ears in a style which we called "cootie garages". She would never play a piece for me so I could get the rhythm and the cadence of the music. This drove me crazy because I could never play with any emotion when I didn't hear it played properly first. I played like a metronome. Now that I think about it, perhaps she was a cipher and couldn't play the piano at all. Who knew?

Towards the end of my lessons with her she had a recital in the basement of a local church. I had to play "The Waltz of the Flowers" from Tchaikovsky's "Nutcracker Suite." I knew the piece perfectly, but felt terribly nervous about performing in front of an audience. The piano itself was hugely intimidating – it was big enough for two or three people to hide in. Half way through the piece I lost my place, and in the silence that ensued, Miss Wright called out,

"Start over from the Andante!"

27

Breathing harder, with sweaty palms and a lurching heart, I started over, but then it happened again at the same place. And a third time! I was a wreck by then, and finally I pushed the bench back and stood up.

The audience applauded wildly because they were so glad the torture was over.

Mum hired a new teacher in the fall. His name was Desmond Ritchie and was recommended by a neighbor as a person who could teach his students to play by ear, using a chording method.

Mr. Ritchie was a large uncouth character, and he made my mother very nervous indeed. She would never leave the house when I had my lesson. In the winter he drove a Morris Mini Minor, painted dull brown, shiny red and shiny black. It made a lot of noise coming up the street, revving and clutching and billowing smoke. In good weather he rode a huge motorcycle and with it he wore a snowsuit, which covered every inch of him. It was an ugly mustard-brown color, lined with blue and white striped pajama flannel, which poked through holes in many places. He was quite the sight with goggles, gloves to the elbows, boots, scarf, a helmet, and "The Amazing Space-man Flying Suit with warts" as Annie called it. Miles of zippers held it all together, and it took him at least five minutes to free himself from its confines. His stuff filled the front hall during the lesson.

Annie and John would be getting ready as soon as they heard his vehicle coming up the street." Mary!! Dizzy Dezi is here!!" they would yell.

"HO HO HO Little Lady!" he bellowed when he came in the door, stomping snow everywhere, casting off his garments, loudly grunting and groaning with the effort.

Mr. Ritchie sat in a chair beside the piano. He was so large that he flowed over the edges, and he had great trouble crossing his legs. He would take 2 hands to pick up one leg and heave it over the other, with more great grunts and groans. The living room had a glass door to the foyer, which was closed for the lesson, and Annie and John would make leering faces, suck in their cheeks, stick out their tongues, press their faces against the glass to make me laugh, which of course I couldn't, because they were doing it behind his back. They swooned a lot too, because when Mr. Ritchie played, it sounded like Liberace without the fancy clothes and candelabra. I haltingly learned to play the world's corniest songs by ear, including his favorite, which my siblings called "How I love to Feel my Organ in the Chapel in the Moonlight." The correct title is "How I Love to Hear the Organ". I was grateful to never have to play in a recital again, and at the end of grade eight, I told him that I was going to play the flute in grade nine when I went to high school. My career at the piano was finished. His career was finished too. He went to jail for molesting his students. I remember being quite insulted that he never put a move on me, what was I? Chopped liver? Years later I found out that he liked boys, not girls.

Grandfather Gourley bought our 30-acre island at Lake of the Woods in 1919. His mentor, George Allan was the head of Great West Life Insurance in Winnipeg, and he knew the ways of the upwardly mobile: which were the best clubs for golf and socializing with the right people, which directorships were best, and where to buy property. Grandfather was dim about such things, because he left school when he was only thirteen, and really had had no experience with the wealthy upper classes of Winnipeg society.

At the Lake 1942

Pop, Grandfather Gourley with John. Arthur, Margaret, Byron, Beth, Gracie.

Mum is in the front holding Mary, and Annie is looking up.

The island had a lovely big old cottage, with 20-foot ceilings, built in 1904. It had vertical tongue and groove wooden walls and wide verandas all around. Huge pine trees and mossy outcrops of rock surrounded the house, and under it were piles of sawdust where ice was stored. The ice was cut from the lake and kept under the house in sawdust until the summer people came, and then it went in the icebox.

There was also a boathouse with bedrooms in it, Gracie and Beth's house on the south side of the island, and the Lookout, a very small but

 charming single room bedroom with a chamber pot. As an adult, it was my favourite place to stay because of a pair of Grebes who came out in the very early morning to sit on a rock. They had great spiky hair and had friendly quacking conversations sitting on the rock in the sun. We could hear the White throat Sparrow singing all day long.

As kids we were completely blasé about "Nature Lore" (which we called Nature Bore) but the stars were never brighter, the northern lights never more magnificent. Terrifying great thunderstorms frequently rattled the windows and blew down enormous trees. There were cormorants, pelicans, ducks of all sorts, loons, Blue Herons, Phoebes, and Bald Eagles in the air, beaver, deer and sometimes bears on land, and Muskie, Bass and Pickerel in the Lake.

The first room of my own at The Lake was called "The Black Hole of Calcutta" because it was so small. I could hear people passing in the corridor and Grandfather often made scratchy noises on the wall with his nails, pretending to be a mouse. Once while he was passing my mother on the way to the bathroom, he said,

"Helen, I never see you without your teeth in."

"These are MY teeth Dad," she said, tapping one with her fingernail.

"I know dear, but you should give your gums a rest sometime"

Grandfather was hard of hearing and his hearing aids just amplified all noise so he often didn't wear them. The family had a dog named Boots and Grandfather always called him Bruce. I yelled at him, "The dog's name is BOOTS!" and he replied, "I know that, but I call him Bruce".

Grandfather's breakfast was always a big production. First he had hot water and lemon, then CPR strawberries (his name for prunes) orange juice, porridge, toast, bacon, eggs and coffee. Fully fortified, he trudged off down the island to chop up fallen trees for the wood stove and the fireplace. He worked very hard out there in the forest and came home all covered with twigs and cobwebs, flies, mosquito bites and sweat. After a hearty lunch, he had a cigar and a nap in his sunroom at the back of the cottage. At five he had a big Scotch Whisky, and he always made a big show of grabbing his chest, rolling his eyes and pretending that it was heart medicine and it tasted terrible.

Before I was ten, I went to the Lake every year with my mother. It was a wonderful respite from Pop, who was steadily getting angrier at the world. There wasn't much for me to do, so I invented games with boats made out of scraps of wood, lots of nails and string. Gracie was always willing to cut the front V with a saw, and then I had a great time nailing all kinds of superstructure on top and nails all around for railings made of string. I had quite a fleet of ships and a big harbour for them around the boathouse.

Sometimes I went to the yacht club for diving lessons, and I was dressed as Eve for the masquerade one year. The women folk thought it would be cute for me to go bare breasted at the age of 8 - with leaves sewn onto my underpants and nothing on top but a necklace of beads. I spent the entire day adjusting the necklace to cover my nipples. I was mortified!

32

Delphine Penner and Mary

We had a big old Ditchburn launch called The Kananaskis. It was 26 feet long, and the front deck, which housed the engine, was 13 feet long. It was a convertible with a canvas top, deck chairs in the back, and a nice bench for the passengers. It was quite an elegant launch, but so long and thin that it was tippy in choppy weather. It got even tippier when grandfather had a permanent fibreglass roof put on it. Ugly too! There were also canoes, a gaff rigged sailboat, a rowboat, and an outboard.

We didn't have a phone or a TV until the year Nixon left office, so in the evenings if we could manage to avoid playing Bridge, we enjoyed Canasta and Ma Jong, and sometimes rousing bouts of Scrabble. Our Ma Jong set was very old - polished Ivory and Bamboo – it felt beautiful, it even smelled good.

Mum always said that the weather circled around our island because it was in the center of the continent. Sometimes it was very cold and rainy and one year, the house on the next island went up in flames because the fireplace had been burning constantly for days, and the timbers supporting the stones in the fireplace caught fire. The kids were out at the yacht club dance that night and they watched from a flotilla of boats as the building burned. It was so wet that the trees around the house didn't even catch fire. That was the summer that I didn't change my clothes for three days because it was so cold and damp. Lucky I don't live in England.

Before we had electricity, and while we still had a maid, the laundry was always done on Monday – our whole week was wrecked if it rained on Monday. We needed a puffy cloud day with some wind.

"All Hands on Deck!" was the early call to get down to the washhouse. First we had to get the fire in the wood stove going and heat gallons of water. We had a big wooden barrel full of soapy water with a crank on it, which we wheeled outside – the crank had a handle like a broom stick and we took turns pushing it back and forth, which made paddles inside move the clothes around. The wringer was hand cranked too – into the rinse water, through the wringer again, and then pinned onto the miles of clothesline strung between the trees. All the sheets had to be washed every week, so if we had 17 people in camp - there were 34 sheets. I never understood this compulsion to wash the sheets, but at least we didn't have to iron them. Ironing grandfather's underwear was very interesting though, that happened on Tuesdays. He wore a singlet, boxer shorts attached to an undershirt in a very large and commodious one-piece garment. The importance of laundry was enhanced by the family's wonderful house keeper Sara Pancratz, who was always up early on Monday boiling water on the wood stove in the wash house, sorting things out into huge piles, getting ready for "the wash". We often had a boat boy too, and he could be pressed into service pumping the washing paddles. After electricity was installed, we had a normal electric machine, and the laundry wasn't such a looming presence.

To get to the Lake, we often took a ship from Port McNichol on Georgian Bay, through the locks at Sault St. Marie, and on across Lake Superior to Thunderbay, then called Port Arthur and Fort William. From there, we took a train to Kenora. I loved the ship because it was like a gracious ocean vessel with staterooms, and there were lovely teas in the afternoon and a piano where everyone sang after dinner. During lunch at Sault Saint Marie in the dining room, we could see the ship going down as the water went out of the locks. The last time I took that trip on the "Assiniboia" was 1958, and the northern lights were better seen from Lake Superior than I saw them later on Baffin Island. They were blue and green and red, and made a sound like a tremendous shower curtain swishing across the sky.

On Friday nights we would take the big boat into Keewatin to meet "The Camper Special", a train which would bring all of our aunts and uncles for the weekend. One of those evenings I met James Coyne who was the governor of the Bank of Canada, and his signature was on our paper money. It was a remarkable evening because we were caught in a rain - a biblical deluge actually - of tiny frogs. They were falling out of the sky and covered the steps, the platform, the tracks, and they were all over the people too. We thought they must have been picked up at the swampy south part of the Lake by a small water spout which let go right then over the station.

Mum had two brothers who both worked for Beaver Lumber, and one would have expected them to have some reverence for wood, but no. They decided to renovate the cottage by removing the bedroom that Mum had considered to be hers. In the remaining bedrooms, they covered up the original tongue and groove with plastic wallboard that pretended to be wood, and lowered the ceilings to fit the eight-foot height of the wallboard. Mum was so mad that she decided to build her own cottage near Huntsville, about three hours north of Toronto. The land she bought was glorious in the fall, with Maple trees yellow and red against the green pines. It had a lovely stream that fed into a smallish lake. At a cocktail party, she mentioned her idea of building a Japanese style cottage, and suddenly she had the now famous Raymond Moriyama as an architect. He designed a charming teahouse with an overhanging roof to protect the verandah, sliding doors to create guest sleeping areas in the sitting room, and a curved Japanese style bridge to cross the stream from the parking area.

The problem was that the cottage was too far from Toronto, we were all leaving home at the time, and the neighbours turned out to be very strange. Instead of flowers around their house, they had coloured plastic pot scrubbers on sticks stuck in the sand. Mum sold the cottage and made friends with her brothers after a couple of years. The people who bought the place called it "The Jones Pagoda".

Our paternal grandparents, Nellie and A.K., lived in a tiny bungalow in Willowdale just north of Toronto. It smelled musty, stale, and like a million dead cigarettes in a galvanized pail full of sand. The pail sat beside my grandmother's chair, and it was only emptied under duress. The last time I remember seeing them alive was when I was thirteen. They had an icebox instead of a refrigerator. I didn't visit my grandparents very often, because my mother disliked Nellie intensely. We never had Christmas dinner together, and I never knew their birthdays. In 1954 I went with Mum to visit Arthur and Nellie, but I have no idea what the occasion was. I stood at the door to the kitchen wondering who that old lady was, because she looked so different from the Grandmother that I remembered. She said:

"Who's that girl with you Helen?" and Mum replied, pushing me forward,

"It's my Mary".

Then suddenly the old lady looked perfectly normal, just like my Grandmother. Mum explained to me later that A.K had surreptitiously passed her false teeth over to her. I wish I knew more about Nellie, I have her body type, her hair, and I love everything Irish, especially the music. I think she must have had a difficult life raising two precocious children who both ended up tragic alcoholics.

High school was more wonderful than public school because I met so many more interesting people; I had boyfriends, joined a sorority, played clarinet in the marching band, and then became a cheerleader. Mum was appalled. How did I get to be so vulgar? Then, horror of horrors, I went to the football dance with my boyfriend George, and was crowned Queen of the Prom. I was presented with a dozen red roses, a crown, a sincere smile and a warm handshake. George was thrilled and took me home right away to show Mum, who thought that beauty contests were degrading to women, and that popularity equated with mediocrity. She was so cold and disapproving that George and I left to tell his parents, who were much more thrilled. Maybe that's when Mum decided I should go away to Europe. The bad influence of poor George, whom she correctly predicted was going to be "just an engineer" and the sudden inheritance of money from an uncle, made it an obvious decision for her. She also had friends at the Toronto Symphony Volunteers who encouraged her to investigate Neuchâtel Junior College for my grade thirteen; I had to get good marks, and write an essay about why I wanted to go. I needed a recommendation from a teacher at my high school, but the Principal was obviously offended when I asked him. "I want you to stay here to

37

get good marks because I have to keep up my school average. Besides that, I know about your family. Who's going to pay?" I asked my Latin teacher, who was very amenable to writing me a recommendation.

In the fall of 1957, our grandmother Nellie had a heart attack on a Friday and went into hospital. Mum swiftly took action, she bought grandfather food and a television set, and took me to visit to cheer him up. He was completely distraught however, and went into a steep decline and died on Monday of a broken heart. Pop was living in California at the time. He had been sober for five years, and had a good job designing airplanes at the Convair plant in San Diego. His parents hadn't spoken to him since he had left our family. He came back to Canada for his father's funeral, and when he arrived on Wednesday, Mum had to tell him that his mother had died also. There was a small double funeral with two open coffins. There they both lay in beautiful satin, looking quite unnervingly alive. In fact we could get some great beauty tips from that mortician, Grandmother looked much better dead that she did alive, with curly hair and make-up. Pop collapsed on the floor when he saw them. I had never been to a funeral before, and it seemed so odd that people were so glad to see each other, chatting away, smiling and laughing as though nothing had happened. Merle was driving Pop around, smiling and greeting everyone like an old buddy, but Mum had a special reserve of vitriol for her, and she made it clear that I was not to speak to Merle.

Chapter Three
Callipygian Buttocks

In the spring of 1959, my brother John gave a party in our basement "wreck-room". He was entertaining his maths-physics class from University of Toronto. As I proceeded up the stairs to get more beer for all these brilliant men, there was a very good looking one sitting half way up. He was wearing a pair of remarkable green suede Brogues that matched his grape green eyes.

"You have callipygian buttocks," he mumbled through his beery beard as I passed by. He followed me up the stairs and into the dining room. (I was running to the dictionary and holy crap! callipygian means Venus-like). He casually mentioned to my mother that he had seen a Red-eyed Vereo on the Toronto Island that morning. Mum was a keen bird watcher and was immediately enchanted by this fellow, who said his name was Paul. He asked Mum if he could invite me to go sailing at the Yacht Club where he was working that summer. She agreed, and thus began a most delicious romance. He took me to dances every weekend, we necked in the rose garden, and we sat for hours on the big porch telling stories and laughing with all the great sailors. His family was from England and they lived on Toronto Island, so many weekends I stayed over and enjoyed their tradition of playing music and singing in the evening, which I had missed since Pop had left home. From them, I learned to eat Marmite on toast at breakfast (love does *strange* things to people). Marmite is a dark brown spread that comes in a jar. It is made from vegetables and yeast, it looks like tar, it smells dank and bitter, and tastes of condensed seaweed and soy sauce. Members of the Secret Society of Marmite eaters swear that it is great tasting and good for you. Some English people I know think it was Marmite that won the war. Most Canadians won't have it in the house. I also learned how wonderful approval is. His parents approved of everything we did. Nobody challenged me or made me feel stupid, and in fact I was admired, and always warmly welcomed. His mother B. was a Virgo like me, a painter, and she also introduced me to the subject of Astrology. She was like Gracie. I felt like a plant growing towards the light.

I was going to Neuchâtel Junior College in Switzerland in the fall for my last year of high school, and before I left, I made Paul a mobile that reflected all of his interests. It had a tiny book, a guitar, a sailboat, a sailor's hat, a recorder, all made with balsa wood, plastic wood and shaped with the battery driven manicure kit.

In September of 1959, I sailed with my class on "The Saxonia" from Montreal. On the trip over we met new friends, explored the ship, ate exotic food, and generally partied for two weeks. We saw a hilarious movie about les esquimaux du Canada qui avoir besoin de trois phoques par jour. "Phoque" is the word for seal, but it hadn't been in our French vocabulary till then. We landed at Le Havre, and our first stop was the cathedral at Chartres, then on to Paris, staying at L'Hotel de l'Opera, which supplied fluffy white robes and bidets. We thought the bidets were for washing our feet, and I sent a lovely picture of myself to Pop wearing a robe with my feet in the bidet. He wrote back,

"Thanks for picture of you looking like G.R. Lee."

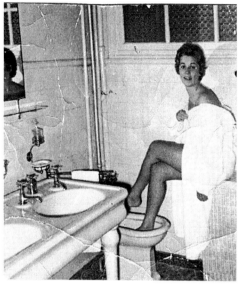

Feet in the bidet

Our pension in Neuchâtel was called La Lovatiere, or The Wolves Den, because it was owned by the Loup sisters. Their first names, Lily and Bluebell were far from accurate. They really resembled twin purple cabbages. There were twenty-six girls of many nationalities staying in the pension, including Canadian, American, Egyptian, Swedish and Swiss German. The mesdemoiselles tried valiantly to keep us in order, but it was hard. We were away from our parents for the first time, meeting European men, hearing Edith Piaf, smoking Gaulloise cigarettes and riding on motor scooters. It's difficult to recapture the thrill of youth, and those ladies were just too old.

In September, some boys climbed up the pillars on the south side of the house and entered the bedroom of Pam and Harriet who, unsure of their French, yelled "Vas-y!" (Come here!) instead of "Vas t-'en!" (go away!). The boys ignored them and went straight to the third floor where the Swiss-German girls had their rooms.

We each had a numbered key to the house, and a curfew of 10 PM. The method to avoid curfew was for the other girls to give their keys to me, I would go home by 10, and I would put their keys on the hall table. When the errant girl came home, she threw a rock at my window and I stealthily went down to let her in. This was a dangerous mission, but the stairs, which were thankfully made of concrete, didn't creak, and the mesdemoiselles slept well, thinking their girls were all safely in bed for the night.

Every Wednesday we went to the Hotel Beaulac for hamburgers because that was the night we were served blood pudding at the pension. We always wondered why it was called "pudding" because it was just a pile of coagulated blood sitting baldly on a plate. Swiss food was always a joke. Forty years later, we still said,

"Do you think this is this veal disguised as shoe leather? Or is it shoe leather disguised as veal?"

We could only have one bath a week, so we shared them; sometimes three people used the same water. Heather used to have the last bath and do her laundry too. My poor father must be turning over in his grave at the thought, as he always maintained that it was disgusting to sit in your own bathwater.

At the Christmas break we took our first major bus trip out of Switzerland, south down the Rhone Valley, through Nougat and Avignon in France, down the east coast of Spain, Barcelona, Granada, Malaga, Gibraltar, and then on to Marrakech for Christmas.

In Granada we visited the Alhambra, a beautiful reminder of the Moorish influence in Spain, gorgeous mosaics, graceful arches, bright colours and quiet reflecting pools. That afternoon we were driven into the mountains to the west to visit the cave dwellers in Puerto Lumbreras. The cave we visited was entirely whitewashed inside. There were several bedrooms with double brass beds, chairs and dressers, a well-equipped kitchen, and a large reception room, which was empty except for balance benches all around the periphery. We sat on the benches that were an amusing reminder of gym class in Canada. We thought that the chickens running around the living room were very funny too.

The family of flamenco dancers came from every generation, from skinny little kids to fat old grannies whose dresses didn't fit anymore. Their enthusiasm was wonderful. They danced to music on a record player with the volume turned right up. Chickens and dogs ran about, heedless of the stamping of heels and the whirling rush of the dancers.

That night we had unusual sleeping arrangements over a stable. It was smelly and noisy, with mooing and shuffling in the hay. It was also quite cold. Mr. Wilde arranged to save our parents' money wherever possible, and that accommodation was especially memorable.

In Malaga we stayed in a hotel that was closed for the season and because there was no fresh water, we had dreadful coffee made with salt water. That night we went for a walk on the beach and encountered armed Spanish soldiers who dispatched us back to our hotel. Gibraltar was frightfully British, with their High Tea, posh restaurants, English bobbies and lovely stone walls. Tame monkeys hopped everywhere.

From there we took a ferry to Tangiers, and everything was suddenly *very* different. It was hot! Our word market doesn't come close to the arab word soukh to describe the unimagined exotic smells; cumin, cardamom, coriander, wood, leather, hay, camel dung, hot Arab armpits, blood and urine running in the gutters, the sound of hobbled camels roaring and spitting, the hawkers, the Muezzin's call to prayer from the Minaret and the flutes of snake charmers. The men wore djellabas and headscarves; the women were covered from head to foot. Vendors of rugs and leather goods came right up to us and wanted us to haggle with them. Fruit vendors wanted to give us fruit from their carts. Most of the time we had a wonderful Moroccan guide named Mohammed, who wore a red fez and a long blue djellaba. He spoke beautiful French and was dignified and charming. We went all through the soukhs with him.

As a Christmas present to Mr Wilde, we went with him to a service in a Coptic church in Marrakech. The regular parishioners must have been very surprised by this influx of irreverent teenagers from Canada!

On the way back to Neuchâtel, we stayed in Barcelona overnight, and I took a walk along the Ramblas with Susie Allan. She was the granddaughter of grandfather Gourley's mentor, George Allan. We were admiring the Spanish people gossiping on the benches on a lovely afternoon in January. In 1960, Franco's Spain was repressed, and the sight of unchaperoned girls in public was unusual. I am not sure how we escaped from the herd of our classmates; usually there were ten girls and at least one boy everywhere we went. But there we were, just the two of us, intrepid adventurers, enjoying a bit of freedom, when we noticed two young Spanish men coming up from behind.

"I think they are following us!"

" Don't look at them." I replied.

"Don't pay *any* attention! " she hissed. They came up on either side of us wearing shiny bright blue suits and brylcreamed hair. They addressed us in every language they knew, French, German, Spanish, Swedish, English and then again in French,

"Bonjour belles femmes, voulez vous voir le cathedral?"

We started to giggle helplessly, and since we were going there anyway, it didn't seem too terrible to accept their hospitality. They were so adorable; they even let us borrow their handkerchiefs to put on our heads while we were inside the church. Then they explained that they needed dates for a party that afternoon. We knew better, but we said, "Sure, Let's go!"

Of course this was *so* against the rules. Our principal, Mr. Wilde, had warned us about the white slave trade. We had heard *true stories* about nice Canadian women being stabbed through the skirt into their behinds by a needle full of Pentathol, then they were carried off to a harem where they were forced into a lifetime of slavery to some swarthy corrupt third world individual wearing a Khafia. But it was such a beautiful day, these young men were well dressed and they did not seem to harbour any evil intentions.

The party was held in a village hall and only a little time passed before we both realized, "Ohmigod we're at a native wedding!" We had exotic spicy Moroccan rice dishes with fish, lamb, squid, shrimp, eggplant, tomatoes, wonderful breads, figs, dates, oranges, pastries and cakes. I remember thinking that it was very unlikely that the food was poisoned and it was so much more interesting than the dour food of Switzerland. Susie and I were greatly admired by the men, they all wanted to dance with us, we kept looking at each other as we danced, and bursting into giggles. Finally we had to go because of check-in time, and dinner with the school group. Our escorts gallantly led us back to our hotel, I am sure we would still be lost there if they hadn't taken us back through the streets.

Our school was leaving for Switzerland the next day, so we would never see them again. Our punishment was that we couldn't tell a soul about our naughty adventure!

We were introduced to Italy at Easter, where in Assisi we saw the re-enactment of Jesus carrying his cross to Calvary. Our school principal Mr. Wilde, was a Catholic Englishman who looked like a muffin. Fascinated by Hitler's girlfriend Eva Braun, we thought he had been in love with her. Wilde had been studying in Germany when war broke out, and actually witnessed Hitler's invasion of Warsaw. He was never allowed back in England, but he had an interesting life running the school for Canadians in Switzerland. He was a terrific teacher of second world war history because he had been there.

In between the big trips to Morocco and Italy, we went to Gletch, where the Rhone River rises in a glacier, to ski in the Alps, and to eat a venison dinner at a hunting lodge near Interlachen. On another weekend, My room mate Heather and I went to Cologne, Germany on the train to spend the weekend with Escott Reid, the Canadian Ambassador, and his wife Ruth, who were long time friends of my parents from Winnipeg. They introduced us to Germany, smoked eel, and breakfast in bed. It was divine after our meagre pension food.

Big Mary, a girl who lived in the room above me in the pension, fell down during a winey episode, and she convinced herself that she had cracked a rib. She was terrified to turn over in bed because she was sure that her rib would break and puncture her lung. She felt *way* too sick to go to school, so she stayed home for a week. The school sent our English teacher "Rags" to inspect. She looked like a very big vertical rat, and she had an unspeakable stench that preceded her. It was Friday afternoon, and I was standing on Mary's desk putting streamers up on the ceiling, and she was arranging a grand assortment of alcoholic drinks and munchy things. Our teacher was properly horrified, and had Mary expelled.

Before Big Mary left, we had a fondue party in her honour and she lost her false teeth while throwing up in the bathroom of the restaurant. There were rules for eating a cheese fondue. If you lost your piece of bread in the melted cheese, you had to kiss the person next to you, but if you were caught deliberately pushing your bread off your fork, you had to buy a bottle of wine. We did over-do it. The hot cheese and the cold wine tend to create a rather dense impenetrable ball in the stomach, a mighty challenge for the digestive enzymes.

We met interesting Europeans at dances called USI. The boys were hotter than ten-cent pistols, especially when a warm wind called the Fün blew. It is also called the Scirocco and it comes from Africa. In Italy, a lawyer can plead "The Scirocco" when clients do crazy things. A girl had to be prepared. I had a girdle that went from above my waist to my knees, and it was almost impossible to get off. One night it served me very well on a date with a horny guy named Rick. The next night, Susie was going out with the same guy, so I insisted that she wear my girdle. It worked like a charm; Our virtue was defended for another day and Rick never spoke to us again.

In June of 1960 I came home from Neuchâtel without going on the school summer trip down the Dalmatian Coast, because my sister Annie the queen of high drama, wrote to me to say that Morley would kill our mother if I didn't come home and save her. Although I didn't think he was the killer type, Annie was the mistress of hyperbole. John had gone to Vancouver to do his Master's in Oceanography, Annie was married and living in Montreal. She thought that I should be in the house in Toronto with Mum. Annie's real motive for getting me home probably was related to her envy of my year in Europe.

The examination results for grade thirteen came in late August, and it was awful to find out that I failed Geometry. Mum wouldn't speak to me for days. I was upset, and over the phone Pop asked what the trouble was, so I told him that I had failed my year, and couldn't go to University of Toronto. He said it didn't matter at all. He had failed Latin in grade thirteen. He was such a genius that I never suspected that there were subjects that he couldn't master. Mum made an appointment with a Psychologist who gave me a bunch of tests and told me that I had a very high rating in mechanical arithmetic, spatial relations, and was in the lowest eight percentile for domestic and clerical aptitude. He informed me that I should try to enjoy the company of women more, because I was too masculine in my orientation. Joining a knitting circle at church seemed like a good idea to him. He thought I should try harder to conform to his perception of what was proper for young ladies. He also recommended Ryerson's Medical Laboratory Technology as a good course for me, so I enrolled and became interested in microbiology, parasites, pipettes, drawing blood, and peering into microscopes.

Annie came home to live with us in 1961 after her first marriage fell apart. I remember helping to unpack her stuff, which had been delivered to our garage by a moving van. She was so disorganized that she had shipped green garbage bags full of real kitchen garbage.

She had two sons, the older one, John, was five, and he went to a nursery school up the street. Every day when he came home he greeted his brother Jim with, "Hi Pee-Pee". Annie finally got angry with him and said that if he continued to call his brother Pee-Pee, then she would call *him* Pee-Pee. Twenty minutes later she called down the stairs,

"Hey PeePee! Dinner's ready" and Jimmy's little voice came back,

"What Mummy?" The next day John came back from school, walked past Jim in his playpen and said, "Hi *testicle*"

Annie was very funny and bright, but her sense of humour went off the rails sometimes. I remember Mum's reaction to a nice gesture when she was painting her bedroom. Annie who wasn't known for her altruism, took tea and crackers with some spread on the crackers to Mum, who said,

"What is this, *cat food*?" Mum was horrified that she could think such a thing, so she ate a few. It was not the only time Annie looked like a nice friendly person while she got you to eat cat food on a cracker.

My romance with Paul was going splendidly; dancing every weekend at the Yacht Club, crewing with the dinghy guys, regattas at The Boulevard Club, and Buzzard's Bay in the States, fraternity parties, and the graduation ball at Hart House. Paul brought me home at 7a.m. My poor haggard mother had been up all night worrying, but I blithely changed my clothes and went to my summer job at the Public Health Labs. It was love, we even had an equation to express it: ML + PC = Love over zero, because anything divided by zero equals infinity.

John's wedding to Catherine Sheldon was a great event in Galt, just after Christmas. Paul was an usher, charming the family from Winnipeg with his debonair demeanor. Morley gave his blessing to Paul and me by putting his hands on both our heads. "If you two decide to do something about it, you have my blessing".

The wedding couple pretended to leave at about 10 P.M., so that the guests would go home, and then they came back for the family party. Cath's father Bill came up to me very late in the evening, saying that he was very worried about Mo, because he was lying down outside and wouldn't come in. I of course, thought my old man had passed out in a snowbank. It was a freezing night, brightly lit by the moon, and sure enough, from the verandah we could see a big black shape lying still out there in the cold. I hurried across the ice, slipping and sliding across the driveway in my tippy-toe party shoes, calling frantically. I grabbed at the big black shape – it was hairy! It was Moses, the Sheldon's big Newfoundland dog, not my father Morley. He was cooling off from the party. We drove to our hotel in an Austin driven by Austina, who drove on the sidewalk all the way to the hotel because we were too drunk to drive on the road. The car was stuffed with people, just like little cars in the circus.

Annie was starting to get paranoid. Our Mum left us alone when she went around the world with her sister Beth, The Bay of Pigs crisis in Cuba happened just then, and Annie decided that she had to protect us. She demanded to know where Pop's gun was. I had no idea, and she went on and on about what an imbecile I was, to have lived in the house all those years, and not know where the gun or the ammunition was. She found the gun hidden away in a cobwebby basement closet. It was a rifle, I think, and her plan was to sit in Mum's room at the front of the house, and shoot anyone who came up the walk. She was sure that the judge who lived next door would be coming over to get the food that she was stockpiling, and she planned to shoot him as he came up the walk.

Pop was living just north of Toronto in his parent's house in absolutely squalid conditions. He had no refrigerator, just an icebox in which he kept his most important books; the telephone book, his science library, books on statistics and aerodynamics. No horizontal surface was safe from the incredible accumulation of papers, wrappers, letters, envelopes, books and bills. Even the bathtub was full of books. Three of the five rooms in his house were so full of stuff you couldn't even go in there. Don't ask how he got clean. He proudly maintained that he hadn't had a bath in 10 years.

For a few months he had a job near Montreal, at Bell's Corners. His favourite entertainment was to get dressed up like a Frenchman, with a beret a turtleneck, and moccasins. He wanted some one to ask him directions, and when they did, he would say in perfectly accented French,

"Malheureusement, je ne parle pas Francais"

(Unfortunately, I do not speak French)

He was working on some designs for drafting tables using negative springs. He also talked a lot about his invention, which he called "The Sieve" a combination of logic machines and diagrams and combinational wheels. It was a method of sorting things with several characteristics to find the most important one. His usual example was of five women, all attractive for different reasons. He rated them for beauty, brains, sense of humour, sensuality and domestic abilities. When he put them through the sieve, he could discover which was the most desirable. He also worked on a perpetual motion machine using magnets. I wish he had had the lightweight rare-earth magnets that we can buy today, because his machine was too heavy.

I loved taking Paul to visit Pop, because they were both so bright and loved to talk about physics. The sparks would fly in their conversation and I would be completely lost after the first sentence.

51

When we arrived at his house, Pop would throw his arms up over his head and holler,

"Mary Mother of God you old pig fucker!!" which I thought was very funny, but there weren't many people that I wanted to come with me on visits, and I was afraid to go by myself. Once he made me a tiny primitive drill out of a popsicle stick, a piece of string and a pointed stick. He had some nice brass circles from the junk yard, into which I drilled holes, and we made a charming mobile out of the little discs, hung by monofilament. We made Möbius loops. Take a strip of paper about an inch wide and 6 inches long, turn it once and glue the ends. The Möbius strip has only one edge and one surface. Cutting it in two or three is fun too; it makes two intersecting loops. He made mobiles out of cigarette papers and little bamboo sticks. He called it "fart art" because he could make it go around on his own gaseous emissions. I made icosahedrons and dodecahedrons for mobiles out of construction paper.

Since he had no refrigerator, he used small cans of Carnation Milk, and every time he poked the holes in the top he sang to the tune of "Do ye ken John Peel at the break of day..."

"Carnation is my favourite brand

I always keep a can on hand,

No hay to pitch, no tits to pinch,

Just punch a hole in the son-of-a-bitch."

John went to see him when he came home from Vancouver. During their conversation, Pop said, "Oh yeah, you want to talk about sex. I tried that on your mother once, but she didn't like it."

We had fun with words too, we wrote stories in Anguish Languish, and here is part of Little Red Riding Hood. You have to use a real English word to replace the word you want.

Ladle Rad Rotten Hut.

Wants pawn term, dare worsted ladle gull hoe lift wetter murder inner ladle cordage honour itch offer lodge dock florist. Disc ladle gull orphan worry ladle red cluck wetter putty ladle rat hut, end fur disc raisin, pimple colder Ladle Rad Rotten Hut.

Wan moaning, Rad Rotten Hut's murder colder inset; "Ladle Rad Rotten Hut, heresy ladle basking winsome burden barter end shirker cockles. Tick disc ladle basking tudor groinmurder. Dun stopper peck floors! Dun daily doily inner florist, an yonder nor sorghum stenches dun stopper torque wet strainers."

He loved to go to Union Station and make little circular metal medallions for people. There were up to 32 characters counting the blanks for your message. He would think up the message, get it stamped for a quarter and carry it around until he met the person it was made for. One was "Michael Allan is a horse's ass". I never heard how Michael Allan reacted when he was given this token. Mine was "Maroo has callipygian buttocks". (When I was little, Maroo was the name of my invisible friend, and it stuck to me) Annie's was "Princess Anya eats toads"

Paul and I had a good friend Alan, a fraternity brother, who was studying Mathematics at U of T. He always came along on our dates, and seemed to have an unrequited crush on me, so we introduced him to my sister, and voila, Alan had a date of his own. Our

53

mother loved both men, and we had a very happy year. Annie was painting, Mum and I were looking after her kids, and she felt quite safe, probably for the first time in her life.

Then Paul won a wonderful scholarship to Harvard, to study Biophysics, and he moved to Boston. This was very hard on our romance, and although he wanted me to get married and move down there, Mum wouldn't hear of it. Annie disliked Paul quite actively because once when she was rude to him, he laughed and said, "That's OK Annie, you have had a big piece of spinach on your left lateral since lunch." I guess if he had stayed in Toronto there would have been a different ending, but he had a shotgun wedding to someone else, and I eventually did too.

When I graduated as a Lab Technician, broke up with Paul and turned 21, Mum took me on a trip to see Egypt, Rome, and Greece, as well as a cruise on the Stella Maris that went to Crete, Rhodes, Ephasus and Istanbul. The captain of the ship shook my hand, looked deep into my eyes and said,

"I am so *glad* to meet *you*".

He took me on a tour of the ship which included the boiler room, the chart room, and guess what? his very own bedroom, where he poured us a drink, and then proceeded to kiss me and drag me on to the bed. I ran out of the room but the door I chose gave onto his balcony with no exit. I made a very big scene and escaped, but I made him angry. After that he watched me through binoculars and threatened to kill my friend Stewart.

There weren't many young people aboard, but luckily there was a handsome young man by the name of Stewart who was on leave from Harvard as a tutor to a 12-year-old boy who wore a beret. Stewart played "Pictures at an Exhibition " on the piano for talent night. We had a very hard time finding a space for ourselves, but finally found an upturned lifeboat, and were out there late one night when my Mother phoned the bridge because I wasn't in bed. Earlier in her life someone she knew had fallen off a cruise ship and drowned. The captain knew exactly where we were, and he came down and knocked loudly on the lifeboat,

"MISS! You Mudda wants you!" He yelled.

Annie and Alan were married in the backyard of our house in June of 1962. Stewart, my friend from the cruise on the Mediterranean flew in from Paris to ask me to marry him. Paul was best man for Alan, but he came without his wife. My new flame Tom was at the wedding too. Annie made herself an amazing hat all covered with plastic jewels. She was convinced that she looked like Cleopatra. Her car was a VW rabbit named Puff, which we painted like a dragon, and she had a tin box full of money to keep under the passenger seat so it would give a lovely cash money noise when it went over bumps. I remember that gas for her car cost 43 cents a gallon, or about 12 cents a litre. The wedding was lovely, but under the influence of too much wine, I missed most of it. My Aunt Gracie noticed that I didn't look too well. She gave me a nice glass of milk, which I poured right down the front of my dress.

Pop looked great from a distance, getting out of the taxi, a two-piece suit with top and bottom matching. Up close though, the shoulders were so moth eaten that you could see his shirt through the fabric. His hat was a brown fedora, also seriously moth eaten, so you could see right through it too. He had old moccasins on his feet.

Everyone was glad to see him, and I think he behaved very well, except for one thing. As we drove in the limousine through the arches of the old city hall where they were married, Pop said, "There is a terrible brig down there, I was never in a worse one" Thank goodness there weren't more people in the car to hear that he knew so much about being in jail.

I was working as a Lab Technician at the Sick Children's Hospital in Toronto, running an electron Microscope and studying pathological elements of Muscular Dystrophy and Hyalin Membrane Disease. A doctor took samples of tissue from the calf muscles of affected boys. Collecting the specimens was a gruesome task, because the child was tied down and the specimen was cut out of his leg with a scalpel, without any anesthetic. There was a lot of screaming and crying and hysteria, which was hard to get used to, but we were assured that it was for the best, because anesthetic would change the nerves, and we wouldn't get good results. I worked in the lab for a year or so, and then I made an interesting photograph of a nerve cell regenerating under the electron microscope. It looked like an onion cell, just creating a new growth at the tip. My boss wrote a paper on my discovery and never even mentioned my name. "Harrumph", I thought. I decided to quit my job and go back to school. My plan was to get an MA in Science and become head technician, or go to Medical School. I was accepted at Boston University for the fall of 1962, with credit for grade 13 and Ryerson, they let me into my Junior Year.

I was assigned to Towers Residence, which was almost 100% Jewish, and the only two goyishe girls were put together. My roommate Margaret was built like a tank, she shaved her hair up the back, and her mother dressed her funny. She was at least twice as smart as I was, and never had to study organic chemistry or calculus to get a much higher mark than me. She wouldn't help me study either. A

56

disgusting smell began to emanate from her corner of the closet. Not a nice smell at all, and very persistent. She caught me spraying an air freshening bomb and demanded to know what it was for.

Me: "For the stink!"

Margaret: " What stink?"

Me: "Can't you smell it?

Margaret: "Well, I'll pay for half the freshener"

Me: "Tell me what the smell is!

Margaret: "No I can't! I'll get expelled!"

Me: "Well I'm going to report you if you don't tell me. "

She took apart her side of the closet and from under her galoshes, running shoes and rubber boots produced a cage with a terrified white mouse whose name was Timmy. Poor Timmy hadn't seen the light of day for many months, but now that I knew of his existence, he had a much better life. His cage was cleaned for one thing, but it was the nighttime activities that got me. She would flop down on her knees every night and say her prayers with much fanfare, then take Timmy out of his cage, lie down in her bed, and let the mouse run up and down her body under her nightgown. Timmy died eventually, and she replaced him with two enormous turtles, which thumped around the room and put their horrible little claws on my ankles.

It was hard to bear. Finally I went to the Towers psychologist and tearily told the story of the madwoman who was my roommate. I badly needed to find other accommodation. The psychologist said that that would not be possible, but after she found out who my roommate was, she understood the problem, because Margaret had a "reputation". I moved to a very nice graduate dorm in a beautiful old house near Copley Square. We did our own cooking and had a camaraderie of women from all over the world, studying music, religion, nursing, science, and journalism. I still had a very hard time trying to wrap my brain around calculus and organic chemistry, but at least I had a wonderful environment. I entertained my roommate Nancy Roach with bits of trivia. Nancy was doing an M.A. in drama, and she didn't do science or math. She was endlessly amused by useless bits of information; for instance, Rhino horn is really matted hair. Scotsmen have fewer retarded children because they wear kilts, and their sperm is kept cooler. All places on earth have the same number of hours of daylight. At the equator it's 12 hours of daylight and 12 of night every day. At the poles, the dark nights of winter equalize the constant daylight of summer. We went to sleep to the crooning of Frank Sinatra. From our windows we watched political parades with the Kennedys riding in limousines, and children in school uniforms marching in great platoons carrying pastel coloured pretend rifles, led by militant looking nuns. Parades in Canada never looked like that!

My German teacher was vastly amused by JFK's` visit to Berlin. When he said, "Ich bin ein Berliner" the Germans heard "I am a jelly doughnut" in translation, because that's what ein berliner is. He should have said Ich bin Berliner. We were all devastated when J.F.K. died, all except for our Organic chemistry teacher who was a Republican, and who scheduled an exam on the Monday of the funeral. He was incredibly unpopular.

Back from school in Boston for the summer, Mum thought she would give a cocktail party so I could see all my posh friends from Neuchâtel. We were all dressed up and looking glamorous when Morley arrived at the door wearing his shorts and the ever-present moccasins. I opened the door, and he barged right in, demanding ten dollars to pay for his taxi. I wanted him to stay in the front hall to prevent him from embarrassing me by coming to the attention of Mum and my friends whom we were trying to impress. Heather Dewar stepped up to the plate, taking his hand, introduced him to everyone in the room. I came downstairs with the money, and he was out of there without Mum ever knowing.

That summer Mum and I spent a month mucking out Pop's house because she had decided that he should go back to California. He was costing her a lot of money, and was really unable to look after himself. At least in the U.S., if he were found drunk on the street they would put him in a hospital for a while and give him some therapy. His house was a disaster. He hoarded squalor. Every morning when we arrived, Pop would tell us that robbers had come in the night and stolen his stuff. We found bottles of gin in places that even he wouldn't have found. Mum took his clothes home, washed and ironed them before she packed his bag. We put him on the bus and said goodbye forever. He was befuddled, my Mother was glad and mad, and I was sorry that his life had deteriorated so much. A couple of days later he phoned to say that he had lost his address book, was lost himself, and he had no money. He did finally make it to California, and eventually ended up in Las Vegas. They never did divorce, and Mum said that another man would be as interesting as diluting milk with water. My Catholic friend Marilyn had picture cards illustrating the major sins, and the picture for adultery was a milkmaid pouring water into a can of milk, thus adulterating it.

Chapter Four
Virgo Perfection

On July 26 at 7 P.M. 1963, I became the tiniest bit pregnant by mistake. Even though I wasn't religious, I was sure that God was not going to ruin my plans by making me have a baby right when I was on the verge of getting my degree from Boston University. Being a perfect Virgo, I thought that I had never done anything wrong; I didn't deserve to be punished, so it must all be a cosmic joke.

Back at school in Boston, I found a doctor in the yellow pages who had a nice sounding name, Kenneth McCall or something like that. I was hoping that he would tell me that I had some small benign chemical condition that would be fixed in a trice. He confirmed my worst fears, but I still didn't really believe it. "What are you going to do about it?" he asked.

I still wasn't convinced, so I said nothing to him, but I called my Neuchâtel friend Susie at McGill University in Montreal, and she said I could go to visit her for the weekend, adding,

"If you're not perfectly spherical!"

I pressed my front against the refrigerator and I could still get my pelvic bones to meet the fridge, so I thought I looked thin enough to go see her for some advice (at least she knew Tom).

She was having an extremely hectic love life with a Scotsman in a kilt, and it wasn't until Sunday that she had an hour or so of free time. We went for a walk on the mountain, I told her my story, and she was firm. "You have to marry him - so phone. There's a phone box right there. Just do it." So I meekly did while she watched.

He was thrilled that we had to get married, and he started making plans right then. It was early November, we decided to tell the folks at American Thanksgiving when I would be home for 5 days, and to get married just before Christmas.

We told his parents after a lovely dinner at their house prepared by the maid. Coffee and dainties were served in the elegant sitting room after dinner, and finally Tom launched into our news. His father's reaction was immediate. He turned purple with rage and decreed that I would be flown to Japan for an abortion. It would be arranged through his connections in business. At the same time, my future mother-in-law Dee rose from her chair, walked over with tears in her eyes, kissed me, and said, "How wonderful!"

The next day we had to inform my mother. We waited for our maidless dinner to be finished, and as we washed the dishes, Tom said, "Mrs. Lazier, Mary and I have decided to get married at Christmas time".

She dropped the plate she was drying. It hit her foot and broke when it crashed on the floor. This was impossible. She limped out the back door into the cold November night and didn't come back until Tom went out to find her. She was furious and she refused to speak to us. She left a deep freeze behind her as she went to bed. By the next day, she realized that there was nothing she could do to control the situation, and although the frosty zone continued, she did buy me a short, not-white wedding dress, a going away outfit, and wedding invitations.

The wedding occurred two days before Christmas, in Trinity Chapel at University of Toronto. The Provost presided, the organ played Bach, and Mum gave us a nice reception, although she wouldn't let us have a wedding cake because of the sexual symbolism of the bride and groom cutting the virginal cake with both hands on the knife.

The years after Boston University are a blur of babies and odious social occasions being my mother-in-law Dee's acolyte. I wore white gloves to serve sherry to the International Order of the Daughters of the Empire. I was invited to tea with proper ladies to see if I were a suitable person to join some posh club; The Junior League, the Badminton and Racquet Club, and the Granite Club among them. At least twice I didn't join because Tom's sister-in-law was Jewish and she couldn't be invited to join. Dee was a big star in the Girl Guide firmament. For 30 years her husband Jack didn't know that she had her Girl Guide uniforms tailor-made by her dressmaker Madame T. and he wasn't too pleased to find out! Proving once again that it's better not to ask permission for some things. Better to say sorry later.

Dee was known as the iron hand in the velvet glove because although she was petite and dainty in physique, in a house of 4 males, she had her way. Once when all the boys were fighting in the back seat of the car, a policeman walked up to the car, and thinking she had done something wrong, she said, "Yes Officer?" and he said,

" Lady, do you want to borrow my gun?"

A study in sartorial splendour, she had a coat made out of a mohair blanket for those rare occasions when mink was too grand. She had special hats made to match all her outfits, and owned almost as many shoes and gloves as Imelda Marcos. Her accessories were perfect too, among them, a silver Porsche. After dinner one night at The York Club I went to fetch my best coat and the coat-check woman said, "Oh yes, you have the cloth coat."

At home, Dee presided over a tasteful dining room with silver and crystal, baronial mahogany furniture, and in front of her place, a little bell to call the maid. Jack carved the Sunday capon from the sideboard, and usually the whole family was served before Dee, but once he asked her first which part of the bird she preferred. She said she'd like a leg, and he was amazed, "But for 26 years you always had the wing!"

"Yes," she said, "because that's all that's left by the time you get to me."

Part of the conversation around the table turned to various talents we had. I mentioned that Tom could undo a brassiere or a garter belt through the outer clothes, with one swift perfectly aimed pinch from behind. Dee was amazed and horrified at the same time, as Tom leaned over and undid her 5 hooks in a flash, and her poitrine fell into her lap.

I attended many art schools to learn painting, printing, etching, silk screening, and glass blowing. I made some interesting mobiles out of glass tubes at Central Tech. As a lab technician I had learned to use a bunsen burner to heat glass tubes, pull them apart when they were red hot, and snap the middle to create two pipettes. The teacher at Central Tech was hell-bent on teaching me to make birdies and duckies out of hot glass drips, so he never understood that I wanted to blow spheres and thistle tubes and turn them into mobiles. He failed me on the exam because I didn't make birdies. I did make some great mobiles though; the tubes were mirrored inside and hung horizontally, with lead shot weighting the lowest balancing bead.

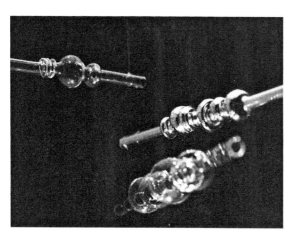

glass mobile

I studied painting at the Ontario College of Art, but kept it a secret from Annie who was aggressive as the painter in the family. Even Mum had stopped painting so she wouldn't compete. I hid all my canvasses in a closet and refused to show them to anyone.

One day a friend of the family who was a painter came over for tea and pleaded to see them. I refused, but she pleaded. I refused again and she pleaded some more.

"I promise to be nice, I won't criticize at all," she said. I laid all 10 on the floor in front of her and she commented, "Well they are water proof you know, you could put your rubber boots on them".

In 1965, after Sara was born, I fell into a deep depression. Wearing a black dress all the time, refusing to go out, I had a plan to kill the baby and Tom because it would be a better solution than all of us living through hell forever. I finally went to Dee's doctor for some other complaint, and he put his hand on my knee and said, "You're not happy, are you?" He knew that I was not cut out for this life of ambitious social splendour. I burst into tears, and he gave me a little lecture and some pills, which I think must have been amphetamines.

With his help, I was back on track for two more kids, and six more years.

We lived in an apartment at the corner of Church and Charles in Toronto, it was a crummy neighbourhood, (indigent men peed in the lobby), but it was inexpensive and it had a bedroom for Sara. On Fridays, my father-in-law would pick Sara and me up in the company limousine and whisk us off to the tarmac, the waiting company jet, and thence to Muskoka. They had a lovely modern cottage with plumbing and electric lights, two mahogany launches and various other small craft. The first summer, Dee hired her niece as my mother's helper, and required her to iron Sara's diapers. Apparently the heat of the iron killed the germs, but honestly, Dee's degree in Home Economics got in the way of real life sometimes. It saved us once though, when we spilled Purple Jesus all over someone's mother's pale green rug. We phoned Dee for advice and she said soda water was the thing, and it worked perfectly. Purple Jesus was a popular drink made of Vodka and Welch's Grape Juice.

Tom and I sailed in a few dinghy races and he blamed me for every mistake he made in the race. He was so rude that I swore I would never sail with him again. The next weekend I sailed with our friend Peter, and we beat Tom. I thought I was a pretty good sailor, with all that experience at the RCYC.

My father-in-law Jack was a curmudgeon in a Saville Row suit with a martini and a Cuban cigar. He loved fishing and shooting and belonged to several sporting clubs, one of which was a fishing spot in the Laurentians near Montreal. It was a big deal to be invited up there for a week, so we spent a lot of money at Streeter and Quarles outfitters in Montreal to prepare for any kind of weather. Lots of zippers, flaps, pockets and vents. The day we arrived blew cold and rainy and everyone wanted to get into bed to take a nap, but Jack was paying for this little jaunt and he wanted to go fishing immediately. To

66

prove what a good daughter-in-law I was, I donned my new wet-gear and went out with him. We had separate punts. I baited the hooks with worms and caught seventeen fish in about three hours. I whacked them on the head several times to kill them. By the time he was willing to go in, my punt was a mess of blood and slime and death, but I had proven my point. He, of course, thought that I was very keen about fishing and had loved every minute of it. The next day I said I wasn't going to fish any more because the limit was seventeen fish per person. I was reading Lawrence Durell's The Alexandria Quartet for the second time, and had a great vacation lying in the sun reading. My lovely mother-in-law had hired a baby sitter for Sara, so I learned how to be happy in the curmudgeon's doghouse.

Another time, he tried to teach me to shoot. It was a skeet shooting range, and there were several stations where you stood to take aim at clay discs which were catapulted from a machine. He didn't know that I was a Dominion Marksman when I was twelve years old at Camp Calumet. I didn't know that I was such a good shot either, but I got 100% of the clay pigeons in the first three stations, told him that it was so easy that it was pointless, and went back to my book.

Pop died in Las Vegas at the end of September 1966. He had been beaten up in the street and left for dead, and by the time he arrived at the hospital it was too late. John flew from Halifax and arrived just in time to hear him say, "Woe is me," as he died. John made all the arrangements necessary and had the ashes shipped to Canada.

Annie wanted to see the cremated remains, so John took the box to sea with him, planning to show Annie in England and then throw them overboard when the ship got into Canadian water on the way home. Annie really felt it was necessary to open the box to see the actual ashes, so a lot of our father's remains ended up in her vacuum cleaner.

Morley Lazier ~ 1963

A year or so later, strange things started happening in our house, bottles of nails fell off high shelves and hit me on the forehead. Dishes fell out of cupboards and hit me in the same place and pieces of linen disappeared. After a week or so, I began to think that there was something funny going on. My next-door neighbour Isabel was writing a paper for our study group about psychic phenomena, and upon hearing of the weird things happening at our house, she asked if she could do a Ouija Board session. She invited another of our neighbours who had a reputation as a psychic, and they set up a board with letters and numbers, yes and no, and they used an upturned glass as the pointer. I was allowed to stand about 5 feet away, and I wrote down the proceedings. First the question, "Is there anyone here?"

"Yes," came the reply.

"Can you spell your name for us please?" and the pointer went to O,M,Y,E,L,R, stopped, and then the same letters in a different sequence, then a third and fourth time. Finally I realized they were the letters of Morley, but not in the correct order.

"Do you have a message for Mary?"

"Kiss your mother", and then,

"Trust Yourself"

The two women didn't know anything at all about my family, and the messages were so concise! After that strange things stopped happening, and I have never had a similar experience.

The next year we went to New York City for a year, so Tom could study some corporate law involving the stock market. We had some great friends there. We especially loved the Freundlichs, who had a place at Bridgehampton, on Long Island where there were spectacular views of the Atlantic, famous authors walking the streets, and the most sophisticated people I had ever met. Through them we met Doug and Deborah. He was a writer, and had asked Deborah to marry him after she put "merkin" down on the Scrabble board. A merkin is a pubic wig, and apparently Casanova wore one. I had a big black Persian cat called Merkin after that.

Our second daughter Beth was born in New York City. Having two small children put a damper on the high life, but we enjoyed Central Park for picnics, and saw lots of galleries on the weekends. I studied glass fusing at the Y.W.C.A. Tom's mother came to see us at the apartment and when she saw that I kept the kids clothes in liquor boxes, she gave me fifty dollars to buy a chest of drawers. I really needed an electric drill though, for the mobiles I was making, and besides that, the little compartments in liquor boxes are perfect for storing little girl undies and socks. I was making mobiles out of optical lenses at the time, suspended from tiny loops of monofilament.

We went to see the musical "Hair" with Mum, and she loved it. We bought her the record for Christmas, and when she really heard the lyrics, she was appalled, and said there were no such dirty words in the show that she had seen. I was surprised that she knew what fellatio and cunnilingus meant. Maybe my finding that out was what made her so mad.

While Mum was visiting us in New York, we were invited to a cocktail party. She was a very well dressed woman, about seventy years of age at the time, and when some young Manhattan whipper-snapper was introduced, he said,

"Nice to meet you, and how do you justify your existence?" She drew herself up to her full height, gave him the 100-watt glare, and said,

"*I* am a *consumer*, I *buy* things, and I keep the economy going."

Shortly after that, I heard on the radio that Martin Luther King had been shot. I dashed across the hall to the apartment of our friends to tell them the terrible news. Whitney, the husband of the family, was trained as a Marine.

"So what!" he said, "that black bastard was a rabble rouser and I keep a gun under my pillow for ass-holes like him." We stopped seeing those people right about then.

Then Bobby Kennedy was killed and there were riots in New York. We lived about four streets from where the barricades were set up to separate the rest of Manhattan from Harlem. I had to take Sara and Beth back to Canada because it was getting too dangerous. On Saturday of our last weekend, we had a picnic in Central Park and used the washroom at the south end of the Metropolitan Museum before we walked home. On the Saturday of the following weekend, several people were shot in that same washroom by a sniper. I was relieved to be able to go back to the safety of Canada. I went to Muskoka with the girls to stay with Dee for a couple of weeks, and then Gracie took a plane from Winnipeg to Toronto, made her way to Union Station, got on the train with the intention of meeting the girls and me at the train station at MacTier, about two hours north of Toronto. Dee drove us

Gracie ~ 1968

from the cottage to meet the train, where it made a very short stop at MacTier, but Dee got lost. We were both quite unnerved by the possibility of being too late to meet Gracie on the train. My heart sank as we arrived at the station, to see that the train was moving. What a profound relief to find that it was arriving, not leaving. The train used to have an elegant dining car with silver and linen. The waiters swayed charmingly down the aisles with huge trays of food over their heads. Whitefish was taken on at Lake Superior and cooked for the second night's dinner. The Canadian Pacific Railway went along the north shore of Lake Superior; the view was wonderful from the dome car.

Grandfather was 90 that year, retired as chairman of the board of Beaver Lumber; he still smoked cigars and kept abreast of the stock market. He read the newspaper for hours, did crosswords, played Scrabble at night and he was grumpy if he didn't get a score of over 300. One night I was up late watching TV and I heard a terrible noise coming out of his room. I rushed in, and discovered that he had trapped his foot in a metal wastebasket as he got out of bed. He was thumping over to the washbasin and choking at the same time. I grabbed him from the back and gave him the Heimlich maneuver. Out came a morsel of beef which had lodged in his mouth during dinner, and which he had breathed into his windpipe when he lay down and went to sleep.

I had a recurring dream about dating Pierre Trudeau. He was a perfect gentleman and would take me to meet the Queen and other important people. Meeting the Queen was truly wonderful, but my insecurity showed, as my teeth got so loose that they fell out. Discreetly I spat them into my white-gloved hand, and then hid them in my pocket. I curled my lips over my gums so the Queen wouldn't notice.

Chrome-plated copper mobile

Ali was born in Toronto June 1969. Sara had just turned four, Beth was one and a half, so I was very busy with laundry and feedings for a while.

I tried hard for a long time to make the marriage work. We had friends, lots of parties; we took our clothes off and painted each other with body paints. I belonged to a women's study group and wrote papers on things that interested me. I wrote about The Pyramids, Acupuncture, early Religions that guided Christianity, Earth Cycles affected by Sun Spots. We went to cultural events, art galleries, concerts, sometimes with my Mum the culture vulture, and sometimes with the kids. I took art courses and became a wonderful cook under the tutelage of Julia

72

Child, even made her wild boar recipe for Jack's birthday. I worked hard to earn merit and respect but the best I ever got from Tom was "not bad". If I said, "I love you", he said "And I you" If the kids made a fabulous drawing he said, "That must have been fun to do". The lack of enthusiasm drove me crazy, so I kept busy in my workshop making mobiles when I had spare time.

Things started to unravel when Tom's sister-in-law suggested that I should get out of my marriage because my husband didn't respect me. A friend of Mum's told me the same thing. When I woke up on my thirtieth birthday I knew that my life had to change dramatically, because it didn't seem to have started yet. Somehow I had to take charge of who I was, and where I was going, because the kinks in this relationship were not coming out. Tom was an eldest child like Mum and Annie; he belittled me to make himself feel better. I was reading Gloria Steinem and Germaine Greer, about feminism, women's rights, and living a worthwhile life with respect, all of which made my life seem strangely irrelevant.

I was waking up from one of my fabulous dream dates with Pierre Trudeau, when the morning radio news woke me up with the information that Pierre had just married Margaret Sinclair. What a let down! As I dressed, there was a political commentary by my erstwhile lover Paul, who had returned from doing a post doc in England, and had become interested in David Crombie's run for mayor in Toronto. His voice gave me weak knees, and I started planning to see him right then. The perfect chance occurred in late Feb of 1972. Annie and her husband were coming to Toronto for a visit, and since we all had been great friends during University days, it seemed like a good enough smoke screen to at least get a look at him.

The dinner party was wonderful (Paul couldn't bring his wife). I looked wonderful too, because I had been jogging around the park three times a week so my husband would think I loved him.(I was actually in training to run away from him).

We invented a silly game that night, called pass the ice cube, which involved passing ice cubes from mouth to mouth, and putting them down each other's shirts and pants. We drank everything in the house and laughed until we were sore. At 6 A.M. I pleaded with them to leave because Tom was about to come down the stairs ready to go for his daily run. He implied that it was irresponsible to have so much fun even though it was Saturday.

In March 1972, Paul and I had lunch, and he whispered that his intentions were not honourable. He was right, but I was adamant that I wasn't going to leave Tom or my girls for him. I thought we might just have a little spring fling, an affair to remember. Paul could be a frill on the side of my life. But that wasn't what happened, because his wife threw him out of the house in June. In a letter written in June of 1972 he said that he had been found out by his wife, felt like a lump of shit and…

"I hereby resolve that we spend an infinite length of time making sure we understand each other so that neither of us ever has to go through this incredible catharsis again!" Expletives deleted.

"It is such a miserable bloody mess! Why the hell did we blow it the first time! I am determined that we shall never have to go through this again... The simplest items of life with you have a joy which I have not known before – there is a purpose, a direction, a whole new dimension to life, to everyday existence that was never there before – how can I be patient in the face of such a beckoning future?"

Avoiding confrontation as usual, I wrote a letter to my family enclosed in a gift for John's newborn son. Mum was down in Halifax to help out. The letter said that I intended to leave Tom and move to a new house with the girls and Paul. John accompanied Mum home to Toronto, and they confronted me. I'll never forget the sight of her car sitting outside my house when I arrive home from shopping. We had an extremely polite dinner at a local restaurant, then back at Mum's house on Boswell Ave., John said;

" Let's stop pussy-footing around here!"

I was put on the hot seat and grilled until I fried, but I stuck to my plan. My mother was absolutely distraught, and wailed, "What am I going to tell my friends?"

A month later, I left home. Tom had given me permission to leave. He always seemed to be mad at me anyway. I thought he'd be glad to see us go. I was disowned by Mum, who called Paul a tomcat, and said that it would be bad for the children to grow up in such a hot and steamy atmosphere. Mum imperiously summoned Paul before her in an effort to dissuade him. To no avail.

I had support from Heather Dewar, my friend from Neuchâtel. She wrote to say that I was brave "because most dummies would go on being half happy until they were too old" She followed this up with "You never really fitted in with Old Toronto Society" and "You have got to be the best mother I've ever met (no sentiment – fact!)" and "You've always been different without trying and you've always needed a Paul not a Tom, because Paul is different too. Anyway I'm glad you're happy at last!" She was living in Australia and her last was, "P.S. Piss on Old Toronto!"

From Annie, in England, "You are grieving because you have failed. You and Tom have murdered a marriage, which is now dead. A dead marriage is just as sad as a dead parent" and then she went on about Pop and his "garbaceous behaviour". Annie contacted Mum and talked her into setting the girls up with a babysitter and sending me off to England to stay with her in Oxford! But I thought that that was a truly bad idea and refused to go.

That summer I went to Sheridan School of Design to study jewelry making techniques so that I could hang my mobiles more elegantly. In a second course I studied plastics, so I could make my own multi-coloured plastic sheets, for making striped fish mobiles. I was hiding from the shit hitting the fan, living in a residence on campus. My favourite person in the course was Annie Mirvish, (Ed Mirvish, her husband, was a famous store and theatre owner in Toronto) who was such a great character. She sang opera all the time, even with her gas mask on. She had a ball being an artist. When it came time to take a photograph of the class, she whipped on a perfect wig, put on some lipstick and she looked fantastic.

At Sheridan, I watched a room full of potters throwing on potter's wheels. It looked intimidating but fascinating at the same time, so I was delighted when a course opened up in the basement of a local framing shop in the neighbourhood where we had moved. I was glad that nobody could watch me, because I made some big muddy messes.

Paul and I were dazzled by joy, filled over the brim with the glow of never-ending love. I was suffused with happiness; the whole meaning of my life had become clear at last. It was as though God had pointed a finger at me and said, "You win!"

I never could figure out who Mum wanted her children to be, but back in those days before the discovery of DNA, nurture was much more important than nature. She felt that people would think that she was at fault if her kids behaved badly, so from her there issued an immense frost. I think Pop felt the same coldness from her. He had given us his blessing at John's wedding, and the message from the Ouija board "Trust Yourself" seemed very pointed right then.

We didn't have any furniture, so we built some. Paul had three little girls too, and they had tremendous fun with my girls on weekends. With friends we bought a farm near Warkworth where we spent hours in the garden, but even more hours plotting against the beavers that were flooding about 40 acres of land. Breaking up the beaver dams in the summer was our favourite sport. By the next day the beavers would have it all patched up as though nothing had happened. We were told they were "bank" beavers, which we thought was very funny because Beaver Lumber money bought the property.

My relationship with my family was approaching its nadir in 1973 when I went to Nova Scotia to visit at them at John's house after Christmas. Annie got incredibly drunk, and after everyone had gone to bed, she chased me around the house with a butcher knife, screaming invective at me. She had the mistaken impression that I had slept with her husband. I barricaded myself in my bedroom to get away from her, it was terrible, but I was jolted into thinking that her perception of me was far worse than I knew. I guess Annie and Mum thought my behaviour leaving Tom was so bad that I had become a complete slut in their eyes. I had to retreat after that, and realize that I was really and truly on my own.

Ron Roy was my pottery teacher at Centennial College the following year. I was working my way up to the more prestigious George Brown College, but didn't want to start in a class not knowing anything. Ron was a wonderfully gentle teacher, he taught us how to think about what we were making, and to plan ahead to the final piece. Details were important, and he appreciated the uniqueness of his students. George Brown College had a great studio, a gas kiln, and good teachers. I met a few lifelong friends there.

That fall, Paul and I attended a conference in Switzerland. It was fabulous to be in the mountains for my birthday, and to meet all kinds of interesting scientists. In September, during the *Festival Des Alpes*, the cows came down from the mountain for the winter. They made a lovely procession with trees tied to their heads and bells around their necks. We wondered how the Swiss could live practically in the same house with their cows and not suffer horrible infestations of flies; perhaps they were stopped at the border by the fastidious police. After the conference we went by train to Venice, then Reika, a boat to Split, a bus to Dubrovnik and then a boat to a marvelous island named Mljet in the Adriatic. It was very far from civilization, and our hotel was an ancient monastery. It was one of those magical places where you can feel the holiness of the earth. I was reading Robert Ornstein's book, The Right Mind about the two sides of the brain and how they function, for a paper I was writing for my study group. Paul was as fascinated as I was, and we spent hours discussing it. We lay on the rocks and swam nude. On the way back to the mainland we had to take an early boat, and it was full of farmers going to the market, chickens and other birds, vegetables and a couple of goats. Everyone toothless and happy; we stood out as toothy, colour-challenged foreigners, and it was quite a hilarious trip.

Chapter Five
Elphaba, the Wicked Witch
of the West

One of the most famous potters of the last century was the Englishman Bernard Leach, who studied with Shoji Hamada, one of Japan's "National Treasures". Leach brought his huge enthusiasm for clay to the west when he started his pottery at St. Ives in Cornwall, England. As he commented in his book <u>The Potter's Challenge,</u>

"We are searching for a balanced form of self expression, and potting is one of the few activities in which a person can use his natural faculties of head, heart and hand in balance. If the potter is making utensils, - simple bowls, pitchers, mugs and plates, he is doing two things at one time: he is making ware that may give pleasure in use, which provides one form of satisfaction to the maker, and he is traveling in the never-ending search for perfection of form, which gives a different gratification."

What I love about clay is its versatility. Like sand, it is created by the weathering of rock, but a pile of sand will fall apart when it is dry. Clay holds its shape because its tiny flat particles, called platelets, are electrically charged and attract each other. It can be a creamy liquid, called slip, which can be poured into a mold, or it can be coloured with stains and painted on a pot. A thick slip applied with a palette knife gives luscious waves of texture. A lump of clay can be spun on a wheel, pinched, rolled into a slab, or formed into sculptures such as birdbaths and art for the garden. When the piece is dry, it is fired in a kiln to bisque temperature, around 1800 F, which hardens the work and leaves it porous enough to receive a glaze. The glaze is applied as a liquid, and a second firing melts it onto the pot and "vitrifies" the clay. This means that all the water has been driven out by heat, and the clay molecules are fused so tightly that the piece will hold water without a glaze. Over the years I studied weaving, glassblowing, cement sculpture, tailoring, painting, and book binding, but clay always called me back. It is magical stuff. Clay is tactile, immediate and primal. The potter is mother to the pot. There are many stages in the process, timing has to be perfect, and the delight in a well-executed piece is like a gift. In some ways, it's like having children, because it demands attention at every stage. Unlike children, it does exactly what you tell it. It can't dry too fast, and for sculptures like mermaids, the parts have to be assembled at the right time or it will crack. I was fascinated by clay and its endless possibilities, and I loved taking pottery classes at George Brown College.

The kids settled into our new neighbourhood in Toronto's Beach area. At the local school, Sara had a teacher for grade two that she adored. The teacher looked like a Barbie Doll and treated Sara like a princess. It was all down hill after that though, because mean men took over her education in grade three, and she resented every minute of it. Beth was a good student and a keen figure skater until she was eighteen, when her coach made her choose between training as a professional skater and going to school. Ali joined the Brownies and they made her a group leader called a "sixer", but she was so dyslexic that she couldn't keep up with the paper work. We had nice neighbours with lots of children, and it was never a worry when the kids went out to play, except for one day when Ali came home and said that the boys had tried to burn her hair off. About four of them had a box of matches. Luckily, Ali's hair was too thick and wouldn't catch on fire. She was completely unperturbed. I thought we should burn another box of matches and then set the pile on fire, in a nice safe environment to show her how hot it got, and how to put out a fire with water and smothering. Unfortunately, the father of one of the boys walked through our front door just as the pile of matches was catching. "What is going *on* here!" he demanded. He was not re-assured at all by my explanation, because he was convinced that I was encouraging delinquent behaviour.

The girls went to visit my mother and Tom up at Mum's weekend farm near Mansfield twice a month. On the other weekends we had Paul's three girls, and they had a great time together putting on plays, having picnics on the beach, and going to our communal farm near Warkworth.

I asked my lovely ex mother-in-law for lunch with the girls occasionally, and one time she arrived in her silver Porsche having received the Girl Guide's highest award, the "Bronze Beaver". She was very pleased to show it off, and commented that a rather odd lady was there, receiving an award for having made all the toadstools for the Brownies. It was Pop's friend Merle Foster making one last appearance in my life.

Annie was living in England, and she cavorted with some interesting people. Sir Francis Crick, who won the Nobel Prize for co-discovering the structure of DNA, invited her to a party, and because she knew that they all liked to dance and take off their clothes, she wore band-aids on her nipples. She painted with Christina, the wife of Stanley Kubrick the filmmaker, and she made friends with "Legs Larry" Smith, who sang and danced with Elton John. I had never heard of Elton John, so when Annie phoned me to say that I had to go see "Legs" at Massey Hall in Toronto, I was dumb-founded. She told me to phone the hotel where they were staying in Montreal, which I did, and asked for John Elton. The only other name I knew was Legs Larry. Paul and I saw the end of the concert and went to the stage door. Legs Larry came out wearing a full-length blue satin gown and high-heeled wedgies, covered with sequins, and way too much make-up. I wasn't prepared for this, so when he said that we should go to Niagara Falls with him and Bernie Taupin in a limo to party all night with vodka and cocaine, I suddenly felt way too square. I said I had three kids and a babysitter. I had to go home.

In April 1974, Paul and I had a party at our house, and he introduced me to a woman I came to detest. I'll call her Elphaba, the Wicked Witch of the West. She was a postdoctoral student from Australia who worked in Paul's lab, and it became evident that there was a pretty serious connection between them. She lent him a lot of books, including "Open Marriage" by George and Nena O'Neill. It advocated a lifestyle in which married people allowed each other to have other serious partners outside the marriage. Monogamy seemed rather passé to them. I was offered an affair with her mousy husband, which I declined. He was so boring, it was no wonder she wanted an extra marital affair with Paul. I was heart broken but didn't want to know the full extent of what was happening, so I stuck my head in the sand for a few months. Then one day I queried him, and realized that if you don't want to know the answer, *don't ask the question.*
"What do you do at lunch time?"

"Well we go to Elphaba's house most days".

And that was it for me. I was inconsolable, but he wouldn't budge. Not only did he want his cake and eat it too, he was having my cake as well. My mother had been right. He was a tomcat and I was an idiot. He went to live in a ménage à trois with Elphaba and her husband, and she had a baby with Paul's big grape-green eyes.

What agonies I went through. I phoned him to hear him say hello, I called his ex wife, I apologized to Tom for breaking his heart, I walked in the rain, drove around the city crying to Dolly Parton singing, "Here you come again, looking so much better than a body has a right to". Another hurtin' song of the time was "Never gonna fall in love again, 'cause I couldn't bear to feel the pain of remembering how it used to be". I had invested everything in that relationship, he had sworn undying love, and even my father had given his blessing, once from beyond the grave.

Chapter Six
Gypsy Potter

In the summer of 1976, I took the girls to The Haliburton School of Art so I could study pottery. My teacher was Pony, an ingenious guy who could build anything. He had drive and determination, and he smouldered in a virile middle-eastern way. He was twenty-five when I met him, and we got along very well. I had been lassoed by the love of clay, and he was an enthusiastic teacher. After Haliburton, my girls went to camp for a month, so we had time to ourselves. Pony invited me to work with him at some workshops that summer, and by working as his studio assistant, I learned a lot about making pots, firing the kiln, and mixing glazes. Pony was fiery. I thought he was funny and exotic. He wasn't socially acceptable at all, which appealed to my rebellious nature. I loved his passion and spontaneity, and furthermore, he looked like Jim Croce. Pony insisted that we get married. He was a gypsy, and I was an urban housewife. He was ten years younger than me, only twelve years older than Sara, and he didn't read books. My friends were concerned. This had to be a rebound from Paul, was I searching for love in all the wrong places?

Paul drove up to Haliburton and asked me to marry him. I said no because I thought that the Elphaba woman would be ever-present, like Camilla Parker Bowles. Besides that, I didn't think I could ever forgive him for his betrayal and my ruined relationship with my family. I had sacrificed everything for him. Pony was wild, but he was funny and sweet, he loved the girls, and he was passionate about marrying the four of us. I was flattered. I had to persuade my friends that I was not completely insane. Elphaba sent me a note to say "Marry in haste, repent at leisure".

We were married in October of 1976, and for a while, in the glow of lust, everything seemed wonderful. Pony was quite rational. We bought a building in the east end of Toronto, which was a perfect pottery studio. We had a tenant to pay the mortgage, a driveway, a back yard, lots of indoor space to make work, dry it slowly and then another room for a glaze lab and bisque kilns. He drove a pick-up truck, I drove a Peugeot Diesel sedan, and my CB handle was "Diesel Queen". As he signed off, he always said, "Ten four good buddy; keep the sunny side up and the dirty side down".

Pony's mother redecorated her house because she thought mine was so classy. I had a cranberry red living room and some nice oriental rugs on a dark wood floor. At her house, she put up lavender flock wallpaper with lime green and white gingham curtains. I can't remember what I said to approve, but whatever it was it was a big lie. Its ugliness defied description.

For my birthday that September, Pony bought me a bike and took the whole family to the top of the CN Tower for lunch. Then he decided that since he had a dog, we should all have pets. Off we went to the pet store, where Ali got a hampster, Beth got a budgie, Sara got a gerbil. At the Humane Society, I found my black cat that we called

Captain Shadow. When we got home, the hamster was missing. He had gnawed his way out of the box and the bag from the pet store, and had vanished. Pony took the seats out of the car and there was the hampster, rescued from himself. Pony's dog always ate Captain Shadow's food, so we emptied out the bottom shelf of the kitchen cupboard, Pony cut a hole in the door, and the cat had his own private dining room. One night Beth had a birthday party sleepover in the basement "wreck room" and a terrible screeching was heard throughout the house at about three in the morning. By the time I got downstairs it was too late. Beth's friends were in the kitchen watching in horror as the cat ate the budgie in his dining room. Sara's gerbil didn't last long either. She threw him out of her room in the middle of the night with loud curse words. Gerbils like to run laps in the middle of the night. It was another bad way to learn the word "nocturnal".

Pony and I went to Calgary to do a pottery workshop at the University. While we were away, Charlie Duponte (Ali's first grade teacher at Montcrest) and his wife Johanna stayed in the house to look after the girls. They had a young Samoyed dog named Neige who was about as cute as a dog could get, and Ali loved to get down on the floor to play with her. Pony's dog went nuts and attacked Ali, biting her all over her face. It had snowed a huge amount and Johanna had to take Ali to the hospital on the streetcar because of the state of the roads. Ali had to have about thirty stitches to close up the bites. It didn't scar her forever, thankfully, and she still likes dogs better than I do.

Pony looked after the kids once when I went to a yoga retreat in Nassau. They had a wonderful time breaking all the rules; they ate at McDonald's and Super-Burger when I was away, and stayed up late watching TV.

At the yoga ashram, Swami Vishnu had gathered an amazing group of healers including an astrologer, a Chinese acupuncturist, Edgar Mitchell the astronaut, Cleve Baxter (who wrote "The Secret Life of Plants") and the musician Ravi Shankar among others.

Cleve Baxter spoke about how he measured the responses of plants to threats of burning with a cigarette. The plants moved away from extreme heat. He measured all kinds of things, including the reaction to music, proving that plants are more sentient than we knew.

Edgar Mitchell told us about his cosmic experience, seeing the earth hanging out in space as he came around the back of the moon in Apollo 14. He said that it had changed his life, and he was planning to start a new Institute of "Noetic Science". The only question I have ever asked in public was of him. I asked how he spelled it, and was surprised that it started with "no" instead of "kn" as in knowledge or "gn" as in "gnosis", which is mystical knowledge.

The Chinese Doctor of acupuncture's accent was so thick we could hardly understand him at all - too bad, he was telling the women where to apply acupressure to an impotent man. "Stick up like iron bar!" he said, demonstrating by snapping his forearm to the vertical position.

On Easter Sunday, we were addressed by a Priest from Montreal, Doctor John Rossner. He was married to an amazing psychic woman, and he sparkled with truths of the Universe. He said that God was perceived differently by all the religions, but all roads lead to where He is. Dr. Rossner wasn't didactic about Christianity; he didn't require any formalities of the church. After his talk he led us in a meditation, and during it, I felt myself transformed by light, as if I were melting and becoming equal to anyone else in the face of God. I had an intense feeling of inner joy, and a sudden flood of knowing my connection to the universe. Knowing is different from believing. I didn't tell many people about this experience, especially after Pony laughed me out of the room when I told him.

The Astrologer did Ali's chart and confirmed that she was learning disabled.

I started to study Astrology from books, interested in my children's different personalities, why they behaved the way they did. Life was so much easier when I didn't have to take the blame for Sara's behaviour problems, and it was also a curative thing for me, having come from an alcoholic family where blame is always being thrown in your face. Alcoholics hardly ever take responsibility for anything, they always have someone to blame. In some book I found a quincunx between my chart and Pony's, which appears in the doomed relationships of older women and younger men. That was true too. I should have taken up Astrology before I met him.

Pony was annoyed by all my books. He thought that by reading even the newspaper, I was shunning him. Somebody gave me C.S. Lewis's <u>The Great Divorce</u>, and Pony went into a tailspin because he thought I was plotting against him. The book is actually about the difference between art and science. He was incredibly jealous of every friend I had, even long standing women friends. He didn't like my "smart ass" study group, so I gave that up. If I had lunch with friends, he accused me of "dilettantin' around". After an argument he was incredibly sweet and brought me flowers, but then things went from bad to worse. It started in the summer of 1977 when he went into a jealous rage about Charlie Duponte, because Pony thought it was impossible for men and women to have platonic relationships. Physical abuse was something I was completely unprepared for. Being pushed around, threatened, having things thrown at my head was terrifying. The worst part was that I never knew what would set him off. Once it was a friend phoning me up and saying, "God Mary, you are the most eccentric person I ever met". I thought this was a great compliment, so I repeated it to Pony, and he went into a rage, chased me upstairs and tore the door off the bedroom. One night at dinner in front of the kids he said, "I hate this house, I think I'll burn it down and build a better one with the insurance money". After an evening at Ali's school, he was driving us home in the Peugeot, and he said that he had decided to run the car into an abutment and kill both of us. He was speaking in the present, not the future. I was wearing a long skirt and high heels, but we weren't moving very fast at the time because of a stop light up ahead, so I opened the passenger door, jumped as far as I could, and rolled into somebody's front yard. I carried my shoes, disappeared into the back of a house and climbed over a few fences. He didn't try to catch me, thank God; it might have been the end of me right then.

I had been given a key to the front door of a dear friend's house in case something bad happened, so I went there in a taxi, and hid out for a couple of days. I phoned and said that I required him to move out so I could be home when the girls returned on Sunday night. He was contrite, adorable, and moved back in a week later with lavish gifts for everyone. Did I mention that we had a joint bank account? His theme song was "You got the money honey, I got the time, When you got no more money, honey, I got no more time".

That Christmas, his mother asked me if he was "rough". I said that he was pretty rough sometimes, but it always seemed to be my fault. She said, "I always thought he was just like his father. In 30 years, I have left him 35 times, and he has always come after me with a gun or a knife. You should get him out of there and put bars on the windows".

He left in February after another huge argument. He thought I was having an affair with Paul. He also wanted us to have a baby, but I had been surgically sterilized. (Praise Be!) Pony thought that I wouldn't have my tubal ligation reversed because I was still in love

90

with Tom. Pony put all his stuff into 5 green garbage cans and moved to the studio, but this time he didn't come back. I had bars put on the windows of the house, changed the locks, and that was the end. He lived at the studio building, he rented studio space to other potters, and he stayed out of my way until the spring when he moved. Abusive relationships are embarrassing, the abuser always makes the other person feel guilty for whatever makes him angry, but there's never a road map for the victim. The victim never wants to admit that there's a problem. Like all bullying, you think if you complain they will get you.

We had marriage counselling in the fall of 1977. Pony hated the therapist because he took his shoes off in his office and walked around silently in his socks. The therapist gave us exercises to do at home, but Pony wouldn't do them; he thought the guy was a phony. When we split up, I phoned the therapist to cancel further appointments, and he said I should go to see him myself. At that meeting, he mentioned that his job was to keep couples together, but in my case he would make an exception. "Never let that man back in your life" was his advice. After that I went for "Guided Imagery Therapy" which helped me see my father as a human with demons who didn't have the capacity to be a doting father. I had to lie on a couch in his office, and go into a safe space in my head. I floated to a meadow in Switzerland where I could look across Lake Neuchâtel to the Alps in the south. It was very peaceful and safe. The therapist said, " Now that you are relaxed, imagine a path, and someone is coming along the path towards you".

T: Can you tell me who it is?
Me: Well, no, I can't.
T: Why not?

M: Because it's not my father.

T: Who is it?

Me: I am not prepared to say.

T: You are paying for this you know! What are you going to do now?

Me: I 'm hiding behind a big rock until he goes by."

T: What is happening now?

Me; "My father is coming along the path"

At that point Paul had passed by on the path, so I could have a conversation with Pop about how I felt being four years old, twelve years old, and an adult. Through that therapy I realized that he had trouble in his life, he regretted that he hadn't been a better father, and maybe I should forgive him and get on with it.

The day before we split up forever, I co-signed a loan at the bank so Pony could consolidate his loans, so when he stopped paying, I was stuck with his big debt. I sued him, cringing at one of Morley's truisms, "You can't take pants off a bare ass".

When Pony moved away, I took over the studio building and incorporated Spiral Pottery. I organized classes, rented space to other potters, employed specialized teachers to give workshops in design, decorating, hand-building, Raku firing, and glaze application. We gave classes to children in the summer, and struggled along, gradually getting more people to rent space, attend classes and buy pots. I was lucky to have a tenant in the front of the building to pay the mortgage.

Over 100 students went to classes over ten years. Fifty potters rented space at one time or another, and an insurmountable amount of fun was had. It was a perfect career for me to be building while I was a single mother. One of the great things about that studio was a huge concrete block wall behind the building. Bad pots were heaved against the wall and frustration turned to elation. Maybe they will find my signature there on a dig sometime a hundred years down the road. I infuriated a customer once because I let kids smash ugly pots against the wall. This customer thought we should send them to the starving children in Bangladesh or something. She said we were wasteful; we didn't understand the plight of the starving children... There must have been a deadly sin there –but which one? The deadlies are about wanting more, and we wanted less (ugly pots, that is).

Although Sara was bright and creative, she rebelled at the strictures of high school. Family therapy was recommended by her guidance counselor, but she refused to go. Tom suggested a boarding school in Quebec, but she said she would run away. It was frustrating for me because I had no one to talk to, and of course her father thought that she was badly behaved because her mother was a harlot. It never occurred to him that his other two daughters were well behaved and they had exactly the same parents. My method for parenting was the same as for gardening. I never believed the books by men who worked in lovely clean air-conditioned offices, who never had to change diapers, get cough syrup in their hair at 2 am, or catch cooties from their kids. I believed that children were like plants. They needed room to grow, with light and air and food. Don't step on them to make them feel bad. Most important was to have a sense of humour and know that things could always be worse. It's good to be grateful too, but that's easier after the kids grow up and produce cute grandchildren.

Shopping at Eaton's one day, eight year old Ali asked if she could buy boys underpants. She thought she was a boy until she turned thirteen and it became obvious that she wasn't. I didn't want to be seen buying my daughter boy's underwear, so I sent her down the aisle to do it herself. She came back very quickly and said, "We have to go right now" She was insistent that we drop what we were doing and get out of there. In the car it went like this;

Ali: "Mum, there was a man with his thing coming out of his pocket"

Me: "His thing? What kind of a thing?

Ali: "You know, Mum, his dick."

Me: "Out of his pocket? How big was it?"

Ali: "Showing me with her hands, THIS BIG indicating about 15 inches."

Me: (thinking my God, could Rasputin have risen again in Eaton's? - he was famous for his fifteen inches)

Beth: " What thing, you mean his weenie?"

We laughed and thought up all the names we knew for that maligned part of the male anatomy. Beth made up a poem,

Dick, dicky, wiener weenie,
pecker, pee pee, thing,
Hey Mister, Happy Valentine's.
It's hanging out of yer pocket.

By the time we got home we were crying, hiccuping hysterically and wetting our pants. Sara, who was cooking some American Chop Suey for dinner, thought we had all gone crazy. "What the hell is so goddam funny?" she yelled at us, imitating her curmudgeonly grandfather. During dinner we took turns telling stories about all the scary perverts we had encountered.

One day the phone rang while I was having a nap. The caller was a woman, who introduced herself as Nurse Burkhardt from the Queen Street Clinic. She was calling to let me know that Sara's results were positive. She was telling me that my fifteen-year-old daughter was pregnant. No more napping; pacing and hair pulling instead. The phone rang again half an hour later. This time it was a policeman, telling me that he had Sara in his office at the Police Station because she had been picked up for shoplifting. He was going to book her for theft.

Me: "What was she shoplifting?"

Cop: "Plastic fingernails ma'am:"

Me; "Why doesn't she shop lift a roast of beef sometime?"

He didn't get the joke, and somehow I persuaded him to bring her home for dinner. Two huge policemen ushered her in the door about fifteen minutes later. She went directly to her room and slammed the door. Dinner was a silent affair, Sara's sisters overwhelmed by the gravity of it all. After dinner I knocked on her door and inquired about the pregnancy test. She said that it was a prank, and I was so relieved not to be a grandmother at 40 years of age that I forgave the shop lifting entirely. Apparently, she was apprehended while replacing the nails she had taken, having reconsidered her actions.

A Holistic Cruise

On June 15 1979, I walked down my stairs by the Siberian Iris blooming in my garden, and embarked on a Holistic Cruise, to sail the Mediterranean to see interesting sites and to dance around the pyramids at the June solstice. I thought I deserved a diversion from my heavy-duty life, so I sent off my money and joined the weirdest bunch of people I'd ever met. I flew to Genoa where we boarded the ship. On board were an assortment of fascinating healers, artists and new age philosophers. Our leader was Jack Schwartz, who could stick nails through his flesh. Also on board were, Elmer and Alice Green, who invented biofeedback, Larry Halprin, a famous architect from San Francisco, Zipporah Dobyns, an astrologer who had a PhD in psychology, the Munroe Institute, which provided tapes to co-ordinate the two sides of the brain, plus a woman who was interested in the power of crystals, who had been trained by Rolling Thunder, a famous native medicine man. Patricia Sun, a voluptuous blonde Christian Minister, had all the men enthralled. It was a very California group.

We had lectures everyday on far-out subjects, meditations, Yoga on the deck, dance classes, massages, and a massive dose of new-age nuttiness. My roommate Muriel was an American scientist, and as time wore on, we both got a bit fed up with all this goofy stuff we were supposed to believe. We danced around the pyramids at Giza wearing yellow and white. The dance was a double helix, the Egyptian guys with the camels-to-ride thought we were from outer space. A woman fell and sprained her ankle, and when she asked the leader the deeper meaning of this accident, he said darkly "There are no accidents.

In Bethlehem, Muriel and I were the last to get off the bus for some reason, and a beggar came on to try and persuade us to buy some trinkets. Muriel was brushing him off when she tripped and fell against him, sustaining a slash on her right arm from the knife he was threatening her with. About 3 healers came to heal it, but the cut continued to bleed. She finally found a bandage, pulled her sleeve down and forgot about it. Soon after this, at a fabulous lunch in a posh modern hotel, another healer came up and said that although she knew that other healers had been to see the arm, she was the real thing. She wanted to see the arm so she could heal it. Muriel pulled up her *left* sleeve and said, "See, it's been completely healed, but thanks all the same."

That evening we were having a dress up night and Muriel decided to go as the "Cosmic Turkey". We wrote a poem, which she read in front of the whole assembly later that night after dinner. She wore a toilet paper tube on her nose with crystals dripping off it, some red wattles on her head, and a gauzy sort of robe –maybe her shower curtain. The poem went like this:

> *I am a cosmic Turkey,*
> *Oh see my shining light,*
> *E is for the energy*
> *Vibrating through the night.*
> *She said she was a healer*
> *As she laid her hands on me,*
> *Relax and flow,*
> *And Let it Go!*
> *And I began to Be. "*

We laughed hysterically while writing the poem, but we worried about the effect it would have, so Muriel left the room right after reciting it. Nobody recognized her. The next day Jack got us all together and told us that we didn't have to believe everything they were telling us. That was a big relief because our bull-shit detectors were going off constantly.

Some of the information was very interesting and useful. Elmer and Alice Green were on board and they helped us learn about bio – feedback. We learned how to raise the temperature of our fingers by mentally relaxing the arteries in the wrist. I'd had Reynaud's disease for years, my fingers turned white and numb quite frequently. I don't have it anymore because of those biofeedback sessions. Zipporah Dobyns talked to us about astrology. She was a compelling teacher, as well as an ordained minister and a doctor of psychology. Zip was able to dispel much of the fog surrounding this ancient science. I went to study with her the following winter in Los Angeles.

Tom Hodne, an architect from Minneapolis, was one of the very few single gentlemen on board. At the end of the cruise we had a de-briefing, and he said he'd had a wonderful time and fallen in love with eight different women. This was the era between Germain Greer and the first cases of Aids –things were loose romantically, and the Californians seem to want to sleep with anything that moved. I think I was one of the women of whom he spoke, and it did look as though we were having a little affair, but he was actually my beard, because I was having a flirtation with another American whose wife was on board. I called him Moon Man because he was Cancerian. He was entranced by a möbius loop I made from a torn cocktail napkin. We held hands under his hat, danced under the stars, snuck up to the top deck past the "No Admittance" sign, and were caught by an officer. His intention had been to get off the ship at Israel but he stayed on board for the whole trip. "This has nothing to do with you," he told me. We marveled at Ephesus, where Cleopatra had walked, and the Apostle Paul had spoken in the amphitheatre. It's an extraordinary site on the Turkish coast; there is a large outdoor public washroom with about 20 toilets, with water running underneath, and a fabulous view out to the sea. The brothel is advertised by a little carving in the marble sidewalk across the street. The carving shows the pretty head of a lady, a bag of money, and an arrow pointing to the brothel. Moon Man said the walk was "as beautiful as a Bach fugue" as we wandered down the main street. Sailing through the Dardanelles – he told me he had been there during the war. My God how old was he anyway? I was *just born* during the war.

I wanted to buy some earrings for my daughters in the bazaar in Istanbul. It was an enormous covered market, with lots of interesting shops selling carpets, clothing, and jewelry. It smelled of exotic spices, tobacco, leather and hordes of people. I found a shop I liked the look of, and went in timidly. Three enormous Turkish men came out from behind a curtain, mustaches quivering, grinning teeth glowing in the dim light. They were so pleased to see me that they locked the door! I was petrified, and had a hard time not showing it. All those Neuchâtelian tales of the White Slave Trade came rushing to the front of my brain. They all looked like Pony, and they were terribly keen to sell me some earrings. I bought 3 pairs as fast as I could and ran all the way back to the ship. I bet I paid at least double the price, but I didn't feel like haggling with those guys!

That winter I went to California to study astrology with Zip Dobyns in Los Angeles and on the way, I visited Moon Man in San Francisco. I wanted to see the plaza and fountain he had designed, so I went in a taxi. The driver said, "It looks like a pile of square dog turds to me Ma'am". I had some time to kill, so I went down to Fisherman's Wharf where there were lots of things to see, including a big barking seal in the harbour. I wanted to go back to the hotel by bus, so bought a map and was studying it when a very cute young man sat down beside be. "Are you lost?" he inquired solicitously. "I am so lost I can't even find where I am on the map" I replied, and so he showed me where I was, and which bus I should take. Suddenly there were 5 cute guys surrounding me on the bus, telling me what a wonderful person I was. They could see my perfection and they invited me to go to dinner with them. They wanted me to go back to Canada and bring my children to live with them at their ashram. I leapt off the bus in a panic when it dawned on me that they were Moonies recruiting new members.

The course with Zip Dobyns lasted about 10 days; we learned the glyphs that represent the planets, and the system of houses to contain them. Sidereal Time had to be understood to construct charts, and then we practiced deciphering them. We studied famous people, ourselves, our children and each other.

Afterwards I took the train down to La Jolla to visit my aunts and my mother who were on vacation at The Beach and Tennis Club.

When I arrived, Aunt Beth and I went shopping. "What vegetables would you like?" she asked me. "The broccoli looks good," I commented. "Broccoli is a four letter word!" she yelled, "We have to eat way too much broccoli when your mother is here. We are not taking *any* broccoli back to the apartment." We had been back about 10 minutes when Mum arrived with a big brown paper bag full of broccoli. Beth had a fit "I hate broccoli!" she screamed, and Mum hurled her biggest insult back at her, "Well I suppose you like *turnips* then!"

Usually I had a lovely time visiting my aunts, and La Jolla was a delightful town, but Mum was still mad at me and when they found out I had been studying Astrology, well... they thought that was positively weird.

Ali's teacher Charlie Duponte knew a lot about American potters, and he had asked me to buy him a pot from Beatrice Woods, who was very old and famous. She lived in a beautiful house on top of a mountain, near Ojai California. If I had known how famous she was, I would have been too intimidated to visit. Part of her glamour was that she had been the mistress of the famous painter/sculptor Marcel Duchamp when she was younger. She was still glamorous in her nineties, wearing a silk Sari, little bells and crystals hung around her neck and wrists, and she was surrounded by handsome young Buddhist monks, wearing orange robes. I looked at her pottery in the showroom, her small tea bowls with dark glazes were not very inspiring, and they had odd little labels with numbers. Numbers like 350 and 275, which I thought couldn't possibly be the prices, but she said that her agent unloaded her kiln, and he decided on the prices of the pots, and the numbers were indeed the prices. She said I couldn't afford her work, but she wanted my opinion of a piece that she brought out from her workroom. I didn't say that I thought it was dark and ugly and that the foot was in the wrong place. Oh no, I lied, and said that it was

100

marvellous. She went away for a while and then presented me with a beautifully wrapped box containing the ugly tea bowl, signed "Beato".

Chapter Seven
My Awfully Wedded Husband

Ali had terrible health problems when she was small. She often had ear pain, and when she walked, she veered to the right. We had countless medical appointments trying to find solutions to her problems. At the hospital, she bumped into the wall on the right side as we walked along to the testing laboratory. The neurologist we saw at The Sick Kid's Hospital had her on his knee, and he replied to my comment that she didn't walk in a straight line by saying, "I think she's just sweet." He could find nothing wrong in his specialty, so he diagnosed her as perfectly fine.

She was very tiny for her age, but the endocrinologist couldn't find anything wrong either. Finally we saw an ear specialist who said she had gunk in her head; her ears were infected, and she needed myringotomy tubes through her eardrums. At one point, Ali started to smell terrible and the doctor pulled an old piece of toast out of her nose. Eventually her ear drums were sucked into her head by negative pressure because the tubes got blocked by gunk. The ear doctor decided to open up the back of each ear through the mastoid bone, and feed in tubes with tiny balloons on the ends. The idea was that the balloons would be inflated when in place, re-position the eardrums, which would shrink to normal size, and her hearing would return. It worked perfectly for one day, and then one ear relapsed. Her hearing was too acute. She woke up from surgery in a straight jacket and screamed, "He's a bad man!" meaning that she didn't like what had happened to her during surgery. She could hear tracheotomy tubes whistling on other kids, nurse's shoes squeaking, cars outside honking. Ali was used to being hard of hearing and the noise of hearing in both ears was too loud for her, so she went hysterically deaf in one ear.

While Ali was in kindergarten at the local public school, I went to pick her up for a medical appointment. The teacher had all the children sitting in a circle for story time, with all the troublemakers sitting in front. Ali should have been there too because she was hard of hearing, but she was not in the room, and the teacher didn't know she was missing. I found her wandering on the third floor of the school looking for Sara.

I decided to find a school for her that would have smaller classes and pay closer attention to each student. Montcrest, near the corner of Danforth and Broadview, had affection for kids who were learning disabled, as well as for kids who were brilliant beyond their years. Everyone was treated equally, there were no bullies, and the principal, Katherine Livingston, was one of the most wonderful people I would ever meet. She was not caught up in rules, regulations, religion or punishment. Every morning the students and teachers met her in the big front hall. Usually a bit of philosophy, a reading, a moment or two of silence to reflect on the upcoming day, a song with guitar accompaniment, and her love and good wishes sent them off to their lessons. She wanted a full curriculum with athletics, music, art, respect and equality for everyone.

Every year there was a "Mini Marathon" in the early fall. The kids ran down Riverdale Park across a bridge that runs into a neighbourhood on the west side of the Don Valley. They didn't have to run ten miles or anything, but it was a major event in the life of the school. I was told to be there at 3PM, to bring a blanket, and to be prepared to stay for the festivities. I arrived on time, but as the runners finished the race, there was no sign of Ali. She was only in grade one, and certainly no athlete, but I was nervous, asking other kids if they had seen her. They had seen her sitting on a curb, she looked tired, and maybe I should go look for her in the car, they said. Worry, worry! Were there monitors out there on the route? Did she have to cross major roads? Finally I saw her walking across the bridge. She sauntered across the finish line, which had to be put up again because she had taken so long to turn up. At the award ceremony, she got the first award, hastily put together by a teacher, the illustrious George Poland. It was "The Little Engine that Could Award", which consisted of a certificate, a warm handshake and a sincere smile. We were delighted that the last person to finish the race would get the first award.

At home, Ali said that she had noticed that the other kids had Dads at the school that day, and she needed a new stepfather. There were no likely contenders, so she decided that I should marry the cat, Captain Shadow. She officiated on the back porch.

"Do you take this cat to be your *awfully* wedded husband?"

"I do", and "meow" from Shadow. Thereafter, we were Captain and Mrs. Mary Shadow. He was a delightful husband. He always met me at the bottom of the outside stairs when I came home in the car. He hopped on my shoulder and amused the neighbours by proudly riding up to the house.

Ali did well at Montcrest in spite of hearing problems, several operations and multiple learning disabilities. Her report cards said things like, "she is wonderful, amazingly talented, and incredibly stubborn. She is a real cactus flower". With a private tutor, she finally learned to spell "people" after weeks of effort. In grade three, Ali said she had to go to the Principal's office. Yikes, I didn't think Montcrest had punishment. No fear though, she spent her time in Mrs. Livingston's office showing that her co-ordination was so bad that she could not do cursive writing, because she had dysgraphia as well as dyslexia and dyscalculia. In grade five, a really tough teacher made her do homework every night and she even had to do a research project. The project was to write about a country in South America. Ali was sick the day the students chose their country, so she was left with Paraguay, the country nobody wanted. She read what the Encyclopedia Britannia had to say, and then wrote her piece. It went like this:

"Paraguay is hot and dry.

A lot of Nazis live there. I never want to go to Paraguay.

Bye, Ali"

Montcrest took a trip to the Art Gallery of Ontario and when she got home, Ali, who was just able to see over the kitchen counter said, "Mum, I think I am the reincarnation of Vincent what's his name in the straw hat." "Van Gogh?" I asked,

"Yeah that's the guy who cut off his left ear."

"Well, how come you think you are his reincarnation? Do you want to be a painter?"

"Well I'm deaf in my left, so it's obvious!" as though I were too dopey to notice.

Head lice were a problem at many schools, and the children had to stay at home until the problem was corrected. We used a horrible shampoo with kerosene in it, which was supposed to kill the eggs. It took several treatments, and when she returned to school I put a bounty of $1.00 per nit on her head. Mrs. Livingston wrote back to say "The star of Pediculis Capitis is waning, as for the bounty on the nits, scratch the thought".

Maybe Montcrest was too nice to her. In grade eight she got a great report card based on being on time and smiling a lot, and she passed every subject.

Katherine Livingston had retired from the school by the time Ali was in grade eight. The board of directors had hired a new principal, Mrs. Wilson. When a trip to Stratford was organized, it became evident that she was not in tune with the individuals in her school. Ali went on the trip wearing a baseball cap, and when she gave her name as "Ali" to the person assigning the bedrooms in the nurse's residence, she was put in the boys' dormitory. This was not a problem for her because she never "liked" boys; she thought she *was* a boy. What happened, though, was that the girls had a huge pillow fight in the middle of the night. The teachers were called, they had a head count, and Ali was missing. She was finally located, sound asleep in the boy's dorm. A hysterical phone call at 3AM informed me that Ali was a boy-crazy delinquent, and she would be expelled from the school immediately. On Monday, things had calmed down somewhat, and with teachers and students vouching for her good behavior, Ali was not expelled after all.

High school was another problem, because her marks were always better than her performance. No study habits had miraculously appeared, but her self-esteem was always great. She was admitted to a high school in Scarborough (a suburb of Toronto) where she could learn a trade. She had fun learning baking, painting walls, fixing cars, and doing stained glass art, with no Math, Literature or French. Her exams required no study, and I didn't have to be a harridan about her homework. She was asked to be the valedictorian of her class. At Ali's graduation from high school I stood next to Sara. "What is that music?" I asked her. The teachers were walking down the aisle wearing mortarboards. That was phony enough, but Sara said the music was the theme song from the soap opera, "The Young and the Restless".

My German friend, Frauke, decided that it was time for me to make friends with my mother, who had stopped speaking to me when I left Tom. My daughters went to her farm every other weekend with their father, and I felt as though they pretended I was dead.

Frauke's orders were to phone Mum to make an appointment to visit her, then plan to wear a dress, stockings and shoes with heels: wear make-up, and don't look like a hippy! She promised to take care of everything. She would give me a Vallium, drive me to pick up flowers and then to Mum's house. With Mum, I had a stilted conversation. When she heard that I had broken up with Pony, she said, "Never mind about men, they are so *boring*. In another ten years we'll be keeping them as *pets*!" Dammit, she was right again!

Mum reported that my brother John's wife Cath had phoned to say that John was getting a Nobel Prize in Venice, and she asked if I would I arrange a trip for us to meet him there. Actually, John was speaking to NATO about his Oceanographic research, and he didn't want us to be there for his speech. A trip to Venice seemed like a good idea though, at least for Mum and me to get to know each other after ten years of silence between us. After my visit she wrote to Annie to say, "Mary came to see me today, *decently dressed* for a change."

Annie was divorced by then, and living with Bob in Oxford. Annie had bought a "Baltic Trader," a sailing vessel, which she intended to take up and down the Thames River, renting space to groups of landscape painters. Captain Bob came with the ship. She wrote from England to say that they would meet us in Venice. "You stay at the Danielli Palace, and we will stay in a bed and breakfast."

I was in charge of making the arrangements, the idea was that Mum and I would fly to Athens, take a cruise to Crete, Egypt, Rhodes and Ephesus on the coast of Turkey, and then back to Venice to meet with John and Annie.

The cruise was great, enough food for Henry VIII, and every night after dinner we walked around the deck and then she went to bed. I went to the main lounge and danced with this bossy old German guy. He was a professional ballroom dancer, and although he admired my style and rhythm, he demanded a more disciplined approach to dancing. His wife watched us, and she was very amused. She cornered me the next day to say she had noticed that I argued with her husband about how to dance. She laughed and said she'd been doing that all her life.

Every day Mum would say, "What are you going to wear to John's reception?"

I would tell her that there was no reception, and we weren't invited to hear the speech. "I *know that*, but what are you going to *wear*?"

The opulence of the Danielli Palace was incredible. The Royal Britannia was berthed in the Grand Canal in front of the hotel. The Queen Mother was aboard on some official mission. Our suite had a huge dressing room, a baronial bath, two gorgeous bedrooms and a view of the Grand Canal. Mum took a nap the first day, so I took a walk around town and ran into John. He was making plans to take us to the island of Torcello the next day, traveling by Vaporetto. It was an ambitious plan, using many different numbered boats in order, involving much embarking and disembarking with our elderly mother. On Torcello we had a wonderful lunch at the famous Harry's Bar, and we saw St Mark's Cathedral, which has a primitive mosaic floor made out of different coloured beach rocks. It was so beautiful I just wanted to sleep on it.

The day we left Venice, Mum had a migraine, so I had to manage the bill, which was seven-and-a-half million Lire. All those zeros were a bit daunting, but that included a couple of dinners in the restaurant and two night's accommodation. The trip to and from the airport in the hotel's mahogany launch was also included. When we had dinner in the restaurant overlooking the Grand Canal, the waiter asked where we were from. I told him we were Canadian, and he said that charming Mr.Trudeau and his sons had sat at our table the previous week.

Before flying back to Canada we visited some friends in London, and Annie and Bob met us there, because they didn't get to Venice. Our friends John and Dan lent their bedroom to us, and Mum crashed immediately. There were so many mirrors in the room that she was too embarrassed to take off her clothes, so she slept in them. Downstairs the wine flowed, and unable to keep up, I went to bed. As I slid between the sheets, Mum sat bolt upright and yelled "Bugger Bugger Bugger!" and then passed out again.

Poor Dan had to sleep all scrunched up in a two-seater couch. In the morning, looking in the mirror, he pulled his lower eyelids down with his fingers and said, "These eyes have seen too much!" Then he said he never wanted to see Annie again because she drank so much that even he couldn't keep up with her. He couldn't stand the competition. The next day, Dan took me out for a little walking jaunt around London. He bought me a huge bouquet of flowers that was so enormous that when we had lunch he had to ask for a table for three so the flowers wouldn't get crushed. We wandered down Regent Street and inspected all the fine shops. I offered to make dinner, and chose to buy lamb chops. I wasn't in my own kitchen, so I had to use the ingredients available in Dan and John's kitchen. The marinade was warmed butter with all kinds of herbs and spices, and when Dan asked what I was doing, I explained that the melted butter would congeal on the cool chops, holding the herbs and spices on the surface rather than flowing off into the marinating dish. His comment was choice, "My God, you're fucking Einstein in the kitchen!"

Spiral Pottery was always going through struggles with male egos colliding. Some very strange people rented the front of the building. There was also the ongoing problem of no bathroom. We used lumberyard washrooms across the street, and eventually I put in an Envirolet toilet that had fans and peat moss. The theory was that what was euphemistically called "the waste" would be dried, de-fumed, and easily removed once a week or so with a shovel. How environmentally friendly. Just before the Christmas Show, however, the system had a breakdown, and evil smelling dark liquid started to leak all over the floor. The manufacturer told me to clean it out and take the whole thing back in my car. Nobody from the studio offered to help with this gruesome task. That was the day The Little Red Hen became my totem.

Charlie Duponte was also a potter and a big help around the studio. We decided to apply for a grant to renovate the building, which was in rough shape. We wanted a gallery to feature the work of the resident potters, a big space for them to work, a separate classroom so we could teach everyone in the world to make pots. We were aiming at recovering alcoholics, learning disabled children, physical therapists and their patients, school teachers, camp directors, wives, men, mothers and children. The list was never-ending. Our six-panel brochure started off with a quote from Bernard Leach;

"Clay is a silent language in which we are free to speak from the heart."

In the middle three pages, pictures and descriptions of the classes, studio and showroom, and on the back was a little note about George Lazier's pottery in Picton, Prince Edward County. The Lazier Pottery made salt glazed stoneware crocks, pitchers, bowls, water coolers, butter churns and apothecary jars in the second half of the nineteenth century. In contrast, we had modern techniques and intended to create works of art, which would be limited only by our imaginations.

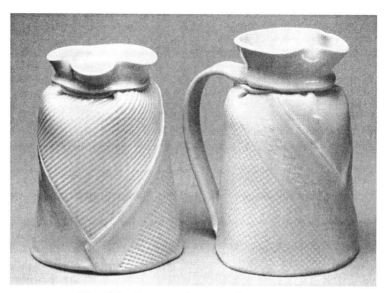

Hand-built porcelain pitchers ~ 1985

It was a great idea, we had lots of enthusiasm, but we didn't see the looming depression of the late eighties and early nineties when banks were charging interest rates of about 18 percent. People stopped buying pottery, potters began to realize that it's a very hard way to make a living; our numbers dropped off, and I had to revert to having a tenant again.

My favourite renters came with fourteen hundred dollars in one hundred dollar bills. Well dressed in suits and ties, they said that they would be repairing pinball machines. The next morning, blankets covered the windows, so I couldn't peek in, but I smelled smoke from cigarettes, and heard the scraping of lawn chairs on the cement floor, but no pinball sounds. The Chinese business next door made beef jerky, four of the workers arrived at the pottery door a few weeks later in an agitated state. They wore bloody aprons, and they still had their butcher knives in hand. Jumping up and down, gesturing with cleavers and yelling in Chinese, it took a while to extract their story. During the day everything was business, but in the evening they played Mah Jong for big stakes. They didn't say that they smoked opium, but I wouldn't have been surprised. They complained that the police had been called to my building in the middle of the night because my tenants ran a "booze-can" with people drinking, fighting, screaming and stabbing each other late at night. My neighbours didn't want the police to find out that they had a gambling den next door. It was also a problem that then I knew about the illegal nighttime activities. The booze-can disappeared after two months though, I never heard another thing. One morning they were gone. The next tenants were bakers and they hooked up the electricity so the pottery would pay for their bill. That was sneaky, but I never figured it out until after I sold the building.

Sara, Ali and Beth

In 1985, Mum wanted to go on another cruise, this time to see Halley's Comet, which she had seen as a girl of 6, in 1910. The Planetary Society was on board, so there were lots of lectures and interesting people to talk to. The worst day of my life as a parent occurred the day I boarded the ship. It was Easter Saturday, and on Good Friday all of my kids had gone off to visit their father while I was traveling. I was vaguely concerned to see them all together in a car that was unreliable, but put those thoughts out of my mind as I collected Mum and headed off to Rio de Janeiro.

It was early afternoon when we boarded the Vistafjord, and Mum went right to bed. I took a tour around the deck, watched us cast off and sail out to sea. When I returned to the cabin, Mum said that I'd had a call from the girls' father, and I should call the radio station. Tom would never have called me unless something ghastly had happened. The ship's radio station had to place the call back to Canada and they said it would take half an hour. I had lots of time to worry about which of my children might be dead or on life support, which crippled for life, or whether I would have to fly back and pull the plug for one of them. It was an unbearably long half hour, but then the phone rang, and it was Sara.

"Hi Mum" she said.

"Tell me what happened," I said shakily, "I'm sitting down."

"Oh nothing" she said, "Ali had a bad dream and we were worried about you"

Sara's boyfriend Andy had placed the call, giving Tom's name when he did for some unfathomable reason.

After that, the cruise was quite fun. It was interesting to study the southern sky at night, and we watched the comet's progress through the constellations of Sagittarius and Scorpio. About the fourth night out, the engines were stopped and all the old people were dragged up on deck at two in the morning to view the comet. They were disappointed because in 1910 it was three times closer and brighter. Even through the telescopes it didn't impress them. The ship took us up the coast of South America around Brazil to Belem and Recife on the Amazon. It was embarrassing to be among the big white bwanas getting off the ship to see the poor natives. They had an opulent Cathedral built out of stone and gilt imported from Europe, and on the steps the natives sat begging, covered with flies. They didn't even have trinkets to sell us.

When Ali was at Humber College studying photography, she met Patrick, who was also learning disabled. Our first conversation was about how many pounds he could press with his legs, and the measurements of his biceps and other muscles. He had the face of a freckled angel, but his multitude of tattoos, his limited conversational skills and strange friends made him seem more like a troll. Patrick's friends dressed like pirates with black bandannas and their conversation revolved around flatulence and motorcycles. They watched TV, and in its baleful flickering light, they ate only food delivered to the door. After Humber College he decided he wanted to become a stunt man. He thought that Sara's husband would get him a job in the movies, and if he married Ali, he expected to inherit lots of money. This seemed to him to be a good life plan. He was so persistent with Ali that she decided to test the waters of heterosexuality. They found a basement apartment close to us and set up house, with neither of them knowing anything at all about stoves or refrigerators. I did the food shopping; I forget who paid the rent. Patrick's style of foreplay was to poke Ali in the arm and say, "Wanna go downstairs?" It wasn't long before Ali moved out.

Mum's memory was obviously failing by then; she was confused and getting paranoid. We thought that it was better for her to stay in her own house with help, rather than forcing her to adjust to a home for the aged at the age of 88. Ali decided that she would live with Grandmother in her house while she went to back to school. Ali wanted to do a course in American Sign Language so she could get a job interpreting for deaf kids in a classroom. She went to the Shoore

116

Institute which helped her organize information, taught her some learning techniques, and encouraged her to keep working to overcome her disabilities. The big problem with this arrangement was that Ali didn't like cooking, and meal planning was foreign to her.

The family had another young friend Elice, who was a great cook, and it looked like a good set-up for a while, as long as I came around to do the shopping and took Mum to her farm for the weekend. I thought it would be nice for Ali and Mum to have a little dog, so I had a very cute little Maltese puppy come for a week's approval. Mum fed it lasagna for dinner and coffee and raisin toast for breakfast, all of which had to be cleaned up off the floor later. The dog was not house broken, and didn't know how to take a walk on a leash. She sat on her tiny perfect ass and had to be towed. Ali tried hard, but she wasn't used to cleaning up doo doo, so the dog went back to its kennel.

In February I organized a birthday party for Mum, and as we were cleaning off the dining room table getting the dishes into the sink, Ali took me aside and said, "Mum I have to talk to you."

We sat at the kitchen table and I said without pre-amble,

"Are you going to tell me that you are a lesbian?" aghast, she said,

"How did you know?"

"Well, it's obvious that you are in love with Elice" sez I. It was unrequited, and Ali spent her evenings watching TV while Elice went to parties.

One day while I was talking to Ali on the phone, she told me that a taxi had just arrived, and...

117

"Oh My God! It's Annie (my sister) getting out! *And Bob*! They have suitcases! What should I *do*? I am locking the door! MUM!! HELP!!"

Poor Ali was stuck there until she found another place to live, which wasn't long, because she was accepted into American Sign Language at Sheridan College, and we rented an apartment in Brampton for her. Ali's ambition at the time was to open a bar for deaf lesbians. (Demographics Ali, demographics!)

Annie and Bob had decided to move into Mum's house with no notice to anyone. Annie had some strange idea that if she lived in the house, it would eventually become hers by osmosis or squatter's rights. They drank and smoked like fish on fire, they relegated Mum to the back seat of the car, and they locked her in the house when they went out. They didn't like visitors to see the mess they made in the house, so they guarded the door like Scylla and Charybdis, and Mum retreated to her bedroom. It became obvious that my services were no longer required, so I backed off until they notified me a few months later that they needed help. I hired a woman named Joan from Seniors for Seniors, and also a nurse to take care of baths and personal daintiness. The appointments were made for the same day, and when I arrived, Annie and Bob were out. I had to clean off an assortment of papers, wrappers, dirty plates, dead flowers, and full ashtrays before I could get to the kitchen table which had to be washed several times to get the grime off. Joan arrived and we sat in the kitchen with Mum, chatting about Mum's companionship needs. Joan was going to come to visit three times a week and take her for walks, have tea, and keep her company. In the middle of our conversation, Bob and Annie arrived, and Bob took up a position behind me, whistling through his teeth as he built up a head of steam.

He waited for Joan to leave, not knowing that a nurse would arrive shortly. He complained that he was the only person who took care of Mum, he was her only friend, and that I had deserted her. He was furious that I hadn't introduced Joan with her last name, and hadn't given him an indication of "her business" there. He raged on about sitting in the kitchen instead of the dining room, then onto how awful our family was. He was unstoppable, so when the nurse arrived she fled, not wanting to get caught in the crossfire.

The next week he phoned Cath, (John's wife) and asked in a tiny voice if he had done something wrong. (Thank Heaven I hadn't told Cath about his bad behaviour) He said "The Bath Police" were coming, and the nurse should be instructed to call Mum Mrs. Lazier instead of Helen. Cath was to tell this to me, so I could tell Annie, who would tell the nurse. Did I say that he was crazy?

Annie had more nerve than a toothache, and she hired a lawyer to serve legal papers suing us for commiteeship of Mum's person and her estate. I had power of attorney, which Annie resented because she was the oldest. She told the trust company that I had stolen $200,000 that she considered to be missing from the bank. Mum had been supporting Annie's two sons, one of their wives, and two of her grandchildren. Mum had also set one of Annie's sons up in business, paid for his honeymoon in Europe. My ally was Mum's doctor, who said that Annie was a chronic alcoholic and had come to her office raving about how evil I was. The trust company believed Annie until we had a meeting with them and the lawyer who made it clear that if Mum had given me power of attorney, then that held over Annie's crazy notions.

Sara was through with playing bridge and drinking beer at Trent University, and when she got "rusticated", she took a course in

119

real estate, then bar tending, and at the end of 1987, decided to get married. She wanted 5 bridesmaids, so we got busy choosing fabrics and patterns. I set up 2 sewing machines in the dining room and went in to high gear sewing six outfits. I made the wedding dress with a princess line pattern, and the top and sleeves were beautiful lace. When I tried it on her, the sleeves were about five inches too short. That was the only major mistake, a bit expensive, but easy enough to fix. The whole thing went off very well, nobody noticed that there were more buttons than buttonholes, and in the pictures I am grinning as though I have swallowed quite a few canaries.

Sara and her bridesmaids

Sara was very concerned about where people would sit for the dinner, and she spent hours trying to make a seating plan which had the two families sitting together nicely. It was not easy mixing the waspy Martinis with the Italian Olive Oil, and even as she was having her hair done at the dining room table, she was fretting about the seating plan.

In January of 1988 there was a bad snowstorm in PEI, and my friend Juliet, who was visiting a man down east, had her flight back to

Toronto canceled. As they waited out the storm, a visitor named Mark came by as he returned from taking his sons back to their mother after the weekend. It seemed interesting to Juliet that he was a computer scientist who had also been a potter. She heard that he was going to Toronto for a convention at the end of the month, so she invited him for dinner. She invited me too. I made a great veal stew, and took a porcelain pitcher with me to show my work which reflects my personality quite well. It is pragmatic, functional and straightforward, in a unique and simple way. We had a lovely dinner, and then played Trivial Pursuit, which always made me feel like an idiot. I still can't name the four States that start with I. We had great fun, and Mark walked me home around 2 in the morning. The next day I was busy sewing bridesmaid dresses for Sara's wedding so I couldn't afford the time to go out, but he came by with a lot of silly stuff from a sophisticated toy store called "The Last Wind-up". That night we went to visit Spiral Pottery and then met Juliet and her gang at a local restaurant. First we talked at the bar, and he told me about a Shakti-pat experience. This was an experience of enlightenment which happened at his Yoga Ashram and it was similar to the experience I had had in Nassau at the Shivananda retreat on Easter Sunday years before. This seemed really significant because the only other time I'd told anyone about my experience, I had been laughed out of the room. We played a great game of charades that night at Juliet's house, and then he was gone, back to Prince Edward Island, where he was a computer science teacher at Holland College. We corresponded by mail and telephone, and I made a trip or two down to see him. Mark lived in a rooming house owned by a strange guy who built a huge top story on a heritage house without permission. The landlord was always in trouble with unpaid bills, and other infractions of city rules. The house was constantly under construction, with water pipes running through the railings of the staircase, lath falling off the walls, the smell of old wet plaster. It didn't matter to us though; we were out walking on the beach, enjoying Charlottetown, the market, and visiting with his sons, Aaron and Luke.

The Soviet Union

One of the benefits of teaching pottery classes is that there is such a wide spectrum of personalities that one would not otherwise meet. One of my pottery students in 1988 was Crystal Hawk, an enthusiastic leader of "Soviet Canadian Connections". I was lucky enough to be able to join her group of about fifteen Canadians from all walks of life, who were interested in visiting three cities in the Soviet Union to meet psychologists, teachers, healers and artists.

Our first stop was Leningrad on the River Neva, reminiscent of the great cities of Europe because of its wide avenues, canals and magnificent domed churches. The city was designed by Peter The Great, who ruled as Czar of all the Russias from 1750 to 1800. Peter was a marvelous craftsman, much more concerned with design that he was with the affairs of state. Aptly called the "Venice of the North", Leningrad was designed for the aristocracy. It's full of beautiful bridges, elegant ironwork, lamps and statuary. Peter's interest in design extended to boat building, and he even made his own size 14 boots.

The original grandeur of the city itself is still evident, although a bit run down these days. Every foreign group had an Intourist guide assigned to them, paid for by the state. Our guide's name was Anna, she was very good at her job, but she was limited to prescribed buildings, museums, statues and churches. She was very reluctant to show our group anything that was not on her agenda, so it became necessary for two of us to strike off on our own to visit the Art School.

The building was five stories high, with mosaic tiles in the foyer, high ceilings and lovely arched windows over looking the canal. A gorgeous domed skylight enhanced a circular wrought iron staircase, but there were no light bulbs, so we couldn't see very well. We didn't even know the word for potter, so it was difficult to get across the idea that we wanted to meet potters and see their studios. Nobody spoke English, but after a consultation with a few of the teachers in the school the receptionist said, "Nyet, Nyet, Nyet. Return tomorrow". She showed us on her watch what time, and indicated that he would be outside the front door. The potter's name was Vladimir, when we met, he gave me his card, but his last name was undecipherable because it was written in Cyrillic. He wouldn't take us into the art school; instead, he took us on our first adventure on a tram. He showed us how to buy the tissue-paper tickets from the conductor, and how to cancel them by punching holes using a machine bolted to the wall. It was quite an effort to push through the logjam of people, but we had to do it. If we were caught without a punched ticket, it would be as serious as stealing.

Vladimir took us to his studio which was a complete apartment paid for by the government. This seemed amazing when we were constantly aware of the terrible housing shortage. He had three rooms full of books, slides, and about fifty earthenware bowls two feet in diameter that he had decorated with scenes of parks, cornices of buildings, bridges, and the river. He also made some wonderful clay constructed windows, some open, some with transoms, some with beautiful views of the city painted on the other side of the glass. He has won the world famous International Faenze Show in Italy twice, in 1979 and in 1984. He is treated very well by his country, and is given huge commissions. One such commission was in a government owned plant shop on the Nevsky Prospect, the big commercial street in the city. The work consisted of a series of very large planters with pillars and onion dome shapes. They were stamped with butterflies and dragonflies, and the pieces all fit together to make an architectural construction that was quite complex. Vladimir said that he designed work that was made at the art school to his specifications, and then he glazed and fired them at the school. I was very impressed by his success, the support of his government and his ability to use the pottery at the art school to produce his work. He was treated like a National Treasure.

The Kirov Ballet at the Mariinsky Theatre performed several short pieces from classical ballet, including "The Firebird" and a lovely young girl danced a solo from Giselle. After the final curtain, a large number of well-dressed fat ladies poured onto the stage. Although they had lost their figures, we could tell that they had been ballerinas because they waved their graceful arms around, and their hands fluttered like little birds.

St. Basil's Cathedral

One beautiful day in Moscow, my friend Barry and I decided that we would like to go for a boat-ride on the River that winds through Moscow. Our guide, Anna, said that we wouldn't be able to get lunch or use a bathroom if we didn't take our passports. I felt very brave setting off on this adventure, buying tickets for the tram and getting them stamped, finding the departure dock for the boat and taking the trip through the city. The sights were wonderful because all the great churches are near the river. To use a washroom we had to surrender our passports to the guard outside a hotel. He would give us 20 minutes before he came after us. We saw the guards go after some young men in a hotel. Every person in the building was known to the guards, and nobody else was allowed in. We couldn't get lunch because there were no restaurants open to people who were not on tours sanctioned by the government. Another strange thing was that stores didn't have signs, so even with instructions for locating a bookstore, I walked right by it because it had no sign at all. It had windows, but the curtains were pulled, and there were no displays of books. I was trying to find the original story of Baba Yaga, which is very popular in Russia, but I had no luck. I had a Russian friend in Toronto who could have translated it for me, and the original illustrations would have been wonderful to see. Later that day after dinner in our hotel, I met David Graham, who was then married to Barbara Amiel. I knew David and was delighted to see him, but he was embarrassed to be seen at the hotel, which I guess wasn't up to his or Barbara's standard. The best he could do to save the situation was offer to have Barry and me to his room to meet Barbara. End of story, madame was not impressed.

When we got to Tiblisi, a bunch of us piled into a tiny Lada to visit an artist who lived in an enormous mansion in the nearby hills. (The city is in Georgia, between the Caspian and Black Seas) An imposing gate was answered by a huge squarely built guard with gold teeth, and a couple of fierce looking black and tan dogs. Our interpreter wasn't intimidated, but the rest of us certainly were. We were admitted to a courtyard with about 500 clay and bronze statues in it. Most of the statues were of humans, and there were a few animals. There were too many of them to be appreciated individually. This

125

applied as well to the studio inside which consisted of two rooms, each 60 feet long and 20 feet wide. The ceilings were twenty feet high. Each wall was absolutely covered with paintings; there must have been more than a thousand. One huge canvas was of a bare white toilet. I thought it was curious that he had such a huge collection of his own work, because if he were as famous as he said, his work would be in galleries instead of in his own studio. He had painted two canvasses of sunflowers that day, and the palette he had used had mountains of paint left on it; about four large tubes worth of cadmium yellow seemed doomed for the garbage after they dried out. He was a very important political force and was being consulted by the American George Schultz about the American Soviet Summit with Gorbachev meeting Regan in Moscow. He wore a grey suit and really looked like the classic Ruskie bad guy in the movies, with gold teeth, black brogues, pudgy fingers and a very well fed belly. He was a consort of the rich and powerful, and during our visit he walked around conversing in Russian on the first cell phone we had ever seen. The artists we met were certainly at the top of their profession, which was obvious by the way they were looked after by the state. Crystal seriously undermined my humility by telling the Russians that I was a terribly important Canadian ceramic artist, and perhaps that's why we met the ones we did. It's a wonder we met any artists at all because the Soviet Intourist guides are instructed to show the modern Palaces of Science and Technology. We were invited to dinner at the private home of an artist who designed medals. Her husband Lionel had learned English from British recordings, and by reading James Joyce. When Barry and I were introduced, Lionel said, "Do you hunt?" and when we said no we didn't, he replied. "Oh that's blasphemous!" He was excruciatingly funny without knowing it. He had built his house using bricks purloined from civic building projects. As a result, the colour of brick changed about every three feet. Lionel prepared shish

126

kebab for our dinner, and he built his fire from hundreds of twigs gathered by his sons. The twigs were set on fire between two stacks of bricks, about two feet apart. As the twigs burned down they added more and more, and finally they had a great pile of coals for cooking. We drank vodka and toasted art, culture, peace, Canada, The Soviet Union, and friendship between people of the world.

The next evening, Lionel took us in his tiny car to visit a famous psychic healer and his wife, in a gorgeous old mansion with antique furniture and beautiful glass lamps. Crystal amused us for an hour or so by bending spoons, Uri Geller style. She concentrated her mind on the thin part of the handle until it went soft, and then twisted it into a spiral. Everyone was amazed as the pile of spoons grew and grew. Finally the lady of the house asked her to stop because she was running out of spoons, and she didn't want Crystal to start on the forks.

The GUM Store

The trip ended with a couple of days in Helsinki, where we shopped till we dropped. Shopping in The Soviet Union was very difficult, with problems exchanging American money for rubles, and rules about taking Rubles out of the country. In the Gum department store, there were line-ups to choose what you wanted to buy, then a line-up to pay, and a third line-up to get the purchase.

Next door to Spiral Pottery in Toronto, there was a sign-making business owned by a Greek guy named Emmanuel. One day he came into my studio and said,

"Meddy I like to make proposition in private."

"In your office?" I asked.

"Ya" he said, as he led me out to the driveway where it was raining. He said that he wanted me to be his business partner. He proposed that he would buy my building, I would rent space from him, and I would make thousands of mugs with decals for "Tim Horton's" and "Wendy's".

"No, Manuel, I couldn't do that, I would need slip casting equipment which is very expensive"

"Not to woody Meddy, I pay."

"Well I would have to go back to school to learn to use the equipment."

"You smart voman Meddy, no problem!"

It was difficult to tell him that I um...er...ah was an artist, and I didn't think that making commercial mugs with decals was what I wanted to do. He thought this was hilarious.

"Ha Ha Ha! What! You no like to make money?"

"You tink, eh, Meddy?" and the next day he came over again.

"Meddy, did you tink eh? You like to sell me building?"

After that he came over every day to tell me how stupid I was for not listening to him, and getting rich. He finally wore me down, and the offer of $275,000 was so great I couldn't refuse. The problem was that my lawyer was drunk all the time and I made a stupid mistake with the help of Emmanuel. I learned that I should never take back a mortgage.

The bank is in the business of mortgages, and they should do all the work of getting paid.

"Too soon old, too late smart." Grandfather Gourley used to say.

It took a couple of weeks to clean out the accumulation of clay, bricks, furniture, burners, kilns, bisqued pots, buckets of raw materials, plaster molds etc etc and so forth. Ali came every day to help, friends came and collected stuff they wanted to buy, and I set up a small pottery in my basement at home, but I had been hired as a shop manager for a new craft store on Queen Street, so I really didn't think I'd be making many more pots.

It could have been depressing, but I was getting married to Mark at the end of June, so there was a big party to look forward to, and after that, everyone was going to Lake of the Woods for a month.

Chapter Eight
The Honeymoon

Mark and I were married in the garden at our house in the Beach area of Toronto. It was a nice service, but the new-age minister kept saying "Mother - Father God", which I specifically asked her not to. The best man didn't turn up, so our friend Juliet became *best man*, and Charlie was my *matron* of honour, wearing a wonderful Hawaiian shirt and Birkenstock sandals. When the service was over, our friend Bev, who was sitting next to Mum, leaned over and said, " Mrs. Lazier, wasn't that just lovely?" and Mum made a raspberry. We had a Greek feast afterwards, and Mark's brother-in-law took one look at those killer dolmades and the tabooli from hell, and he took off with his children to McDonald's. The poor guy came back for lunch the next day and we were having leftovers, so he returned to McDonald's.

After the wedding, we went to the Lake of the Woods for a couple of weeks, on a three-generation honeymoon. Mum was getting extremely querulous, so I picked her up a day ahead, hoping to have a calm transition. Annie had packed her suitcase, but hadn't let her know that she was leaving for the Lake. Ordinarily, I'd have expected Mum to be happy to be going to her favourite place, but change was an affront. She felt that we had deliberately misled her because she wasn't prepared. I had to take the suitcase out of the car, and unpack it in the driveway so she could see what was inside, and re-pack it in front of her. Gradually I got her reassured, into the car, and back to our house, so we could be ready for the plane the next day.

At the Lake, there were too many people she didn't recognize, and she was very confused. One day she said, "Who is that odious boy with the huge feet?"

"He's my-step son Aaron, Mum, you met him last week at my wedding. Remember the wedding in my garden? I married his father, Mark."

"Why is he wearing that chain around his neck? He's not Catholic is he?"

" Don't shout Mum, he can hear you!"

"I own this property, you know. I've been coming here since 1919, and you couldn't come here on holiday without *me*. I guess I can do anything I want to! What does a person have to do to get a drink around here?"

She stormed off down the hall to the kitchen, to rummage around in the paper bag drawer, hoping to find the Vermouth. It was hiding in a new place, so she gave up, and went down the back stairs singing, "Ruby lips above the water" in her little quavery voice. She sang this one line from Clementine" over and over. Sometimes she said, "Voici l'hippopotam" every ten minutes. She couldn't remember anything else for ten minutes at a time. Another thing that she said every morning was, "What's for today Saint Peter?"

Mark's reply was, "Just a bit of harping I guess." and she beamed because nobody had gotten the right answer before. The original joke ended with "harpin'! More goddam harpin'!"

Sara and her husband Andy decided to drive to Lake of the Woods in a convoy with friends. They had fun camping for two or three nights on the way, and arrived at the island hoping that they would be warmly welcomed. The boys set up tents on the south side, and the girls came in to say hello. Mum was alarmed. She stared out the south window with beady eyes. She was strutting around like a bantam rooster.

> *"Who are those men out there putting up tents! Are they ship wrecked? Who are they! Mary, do something! Well? What are you going to do?"*

No amount of explaining worked. She would get distracted, have a cup of tea and relax a bit, but then inevitably she'd be over at the window, furious all over again,

> *"Now they are poking holes in the island! Don't they know that the soil is thin? If they put holes in the island we'll all sink!"*

The girls were allowed to sleep in the cottage, but the boys went into army mode, fishing for food, living in the tent and making quick forays into the house for buns. They had beer provisions for a week but left after three days.

About fifteen times a day Mum toured around the property looking for familiarity. The ancient rocks and mosses gave her a sense of permanence and order. It was reassuring that the view down the lake had been the same ever since she could remember, and the cottage was built in 1904, the year she was born. She actually hugged and kissed her favourite old White Pines like dear friends when she met them beside the path.

Change caused her great anxiety, perhaps because she was reminded that she wasn't making the decisions anymore.

We called her walk the "Warpath" because she always found somebody doing something that she thought was terribly dangerous or annoying. It was impossible to predict what would make her angry, because she made up rules as she went along. Swimming too long, playing Badminton, lying in the sun, reading the wrong book, playing the radio, laughing too much and wearing headphones were all serious infractions. Because of her deep anxieties about everything, we had to be very clever to stay out of trouble with her so we could enjoy our holiday. We invented "The Alfred E. Neuman Society for the Preservation of Family Sanity." Since I was the filling in the sandwich between Mum and the rest of the family, I was elected "Alfreda, Patron Saint of the Island". Our motto was, "What me worry?" Our mantra was, " Alfreda...Alfreda...Alfreda..." As Patron Saint, I could point out offending worrywarts at the least provocation. Anyone I noticed taking offense at her bad temper was chastised and threatened with eternal punishment. When I took offense, Mark always pulled me back to reality by calling me Alfreda. It was an instant signal to calm down, take it easy.

Keeping off the warpath became a recognized art, and John was given a "Medal of Distinction" for spending his entire vacation on the roof. Mark was out on the windsurfer for hours every day, and the kids went to Kenora in the boat.

My favourite bumper sticker says, "Of all the things I ever lost, I miss my marbles the most". Before she lost her marbles, my mother gave me one good bit of advice about life. I was coping with three children under four years of age, and she told me, "It doesn't get easier. It just gets different." This adage was gaining eternal truth as it became harder and harder to balance 12 people in three generations, with one who seemed intent on spoiling all the fun.

We could hear the kids yelling "Fun Police" from the dock as one of them sighted Grandmother gliding through the trees to inspect. The grandchildren called this out to let each other know that she was coming. Sometimes it helped to be warned to quickly turn off the radio, hide a book or the cards. She would walk into a room full of zombies, blue in the face trying not to laugh. She was baffled by this, but at least it didn't make her furious.

Down at the dock she scolded her grandchildren for staying in the water too long, yelling too much, and gave her usual admonition,

"There's too much funny business going on here!"

What an emotional hornet's nest I had delivered Mark to! To me, he was "Serene Highness Alfred E. Newman" an oasis of lotus blossoms, a plate of chocolate chip cookies, the eye of the storm. He was working hard to fit in.

It was 90 degrees Fahrenheit in the shade and very hot work making dinner for fifteen. One of the main jobs of the cook was to be constantly aware of the whereabouts of Grandmother, because one of her best tricks was to turn the stove off as she passed through the kitchen. The oven had been on most of the afternoon, and water was boiling furiously. I was toiling away on the gravy, resenting those people who float in the doorway just before dinner, when my sister-in-law came in.

"You're hot?" she said,"You're probably having a hot flash"

I refrained from throwing the frying pan at her, but I did suddenly understand spontaneous combustion.
Alfreda...Alfreda...Alfreda...

At the dinner table, my mother announced that she had met two young men on the path (Mark's sons) whom she had hired on the spot to "Look after things". Things were not being looked after to her liking. Did she imply that or did I infer it?

During the day there was often a Scrabble game going on, especially in bad weather. Juliet was in the hammock on the porch during one such episode, and a huge thunderclap startled her so much that she landed on the floor under the hammock.

"I fleaped!" she cried.

Within minutes FLEAP appeared on the Scrabble board. Mum was cruising around inspecting, and when she saw our new word she had a fit. She accused us of cheating, using words that didn't exist. She was furious, and took the whole thing personally.

In the evenings we played Monopoly, but we waited for her to go to bed first. Monopoly was a gambling game and she really disapproved. Unfortunately, if she had to get out of bed to go to the bathroom, she could see the lights on in the living room, and would always be interested in what was going on without her.

Our friend Larry came down from Winnipeg, and brought a big bottle of whisky, which Juliet, Larry and I drank on the dock, watching the lovely star Capella in the far north, listening to the murmurings of the water under the dock, and enjoying the clear sparkling air. When we finished the bottle, we threw it in the lake, and then led Larry down to Gracie's vacant cabin on the south shore. It was dark, the path went through the forest, and we were pretty hammered. It was amazing that Larry found the big cottage in the morning before anyone was up.

Mum got up just then, found him rummaging around in the cereal department of the pantry, stormed down to the Lookout where I was asleep, and berated me for not having a proper breakfast ready for my guest.

I had to sit down with her at the table in the dining room and explain that she had to trust me. I told her that she couldn't go to the Lake without me, and if she behaved like that, we wouldn't come anymore. Somehow what I said sank in, and she became better behaved.

Aunts Beth and Gracie ~ 1990

Beth and Gracie invited us all over to their new house on the Keewatin mainland for dinner, and while we were all sitting around enjoying ourselves, the phone rang and it was Annie, who said that she and Bob had just registered in a motel at Norman, about two miles away. Annie had been forbidden by our aunts to go to the island, because the previous year she had drunkenly fallen on the rocks, given herself a black eye, and blamed Bob. Beth and Gracie decreed that Annie could never go back to the island. Beth had phoned me in tears to plead with me to tell Annie that she was not welcome at the Lake, but Annie considered Lake of the Woods to be her birthright, so she was furious at me (the messenger). Instead of begging an invitation, she and Bob drove Mum's car from Toronto and just turned up. The next day, John took the launch into Norman to pick them up. Ali and I were sitting on the dock when we realized what was happening. We decided that it was finally the moment for us to swim around the island. The island was thirty acres, so we thought it would occupy us for an hour or so. We did it to honour Morley's birthday on that day, July 25. Many young men had done the swim, but it never seemed as appropriate as right then for two women to do it. Luke and Aaron rowed the boat to protect us as we swam, Mark went out on the windsurfer, Mum went into her room for a nap, John went up on the roof to inspect it, and Cath made tea for Annie and Bob. They didn't stay too long. The silence was deafening!

Three days before we were to leave, we began to talk about our departure, reminding Grandmother often that this event was to occur soon. We made an effort to remind her frequently. I had been afraid of my mother all my life, so it was terrifying to invade her privacy to pack her things. I had a list, but I had to be fast. I was jamming all her stuff into suitcases, emptying drawers and cupboards, when suddenly she appeared and furiously ordered me out. She would not allow me to touch anything of hers. After a hot argument, we both left, she to find a key to lock me out. I finished the packing and removed her suitcases later, when she was busy looking for Vermouth in the drawer where we kept the paper bags.

By the time we were ready to leave the island to meet the plane, she was losing her tenuous grip fast. From the boathouse we could hear a bone chilling cry like a loon's call. She was hitting herself on the chest and screaming. Coincidentally, I had been reading "Virunga" about Diane Fossey's experience in the African jungle. Fossey had described this behaviour among the gorillas. This was not funny anymore! Somehow we got Mum onto the tiny Bearskin Airways plane that only accommodated 15 passengers where she and I had to sit together at the back. Her agonies made me think I would have to take her to the hospital when the plane landed. She was banging her knees, her chest, her head, and the wall of the plane; screaming and crying at the same time. The alarmed faces of relatives began to appear over the backs of the seats, as they wondered what I would do. There was absolutely nothing I could do - so I did that with my eyes shut. I wanted to kill myself for not having been smart enough to have some Valium in my purse. As things were reaching a crescendo, a note was passed back to me from the front of the plane from Mark, it said, "I love you Alfreda".

In the fall, John and I had to hire an expensive lawyer to prove that Annie was wrong, that my power of attorney held even if Mum were declared incompetent. We had to pay Annie's lawyer's fees, which really hurt, but at least she decided to return to England, where, she said, she had left a refrigerator full of food two years previously, and well, she needed to go back to England because she might have rats in her house there. With her, she took post dated cheques signed by Mum for $2000 a month, a Mastercard which she used, but Mum's account paid, for $2000 a month, and the old age pension made out to Ann Lazier for Helen Lazier. She had a new way of telling me I was stupid!

Cleaning Mum's house after they departed was a huge ordeal. Annie left a taped up shoe box full of scurrilous writings, labeled "Open This When I am Dead." She left spiral notebooks full of incoherent raving. She wrote that she was drunk because everyone lied to her and her mother didn't love her. Among the piles of paper was this handwritten story of my conception. (She was only 7 when it happened, and I am sure she didn't know about the 9 month lag time between conception and birth.)

"Morley was a monster. I have had to live for fifty years with the screams and cries of my mother as she was raped the night that she sprained her ankle. Morley shouted: 'Ah HA me proud beauty! I have you in me clutches at last!!' And other endearments. I stood outside the door, trembling, and when John joined me to listen to this torture, I had to take him back to bed. I think it's time that you knew the circumstances of your conception. And why your mother hated your father. Now go to a therapist. Now understand why I suspect that you are lacking some counsel of perfection."

Annie's problem was envy. According to an article by Jane Ciabattari in "Psychology Today" 1990, envy is based on hate for the person who has something you want. It's aggressive. "If I can't have it, I'll destroy it. Envy can be murderous in its intensity. Envious people live in a perpetual state of anxious competitive comparison, focusing on what others around them have, and what they themselves lack. Jealousy is based on love and focuses on possessing the loved object."

Annie had a Bible with a marker in it saying "God's phone number". There were at least 10 bottles of stomach bitters with fifty percent alcohol content, plus rum, cognac, and gin in the linen cupboard, under the mattress and in her chest of drawers. John came from Halifax to help clean up the mess, and every time Mum went by the door to Annie's room she'd look in at us and mutter,

"Oh God, save us!"

The house smelled so terrible that we had to have it painted and the carpets cleaned professionally. John took Mum to Halifax for the summer where she could let her anxiety subside.

In the fall we hired the only woman available from a Toronto agency, the patronizing Patrona, who was a Jamaican giantess. Patrona smudged the house with smoking sage the first week she was there, because Annie and Bob had left such "bad vibrations" in the house. Patrona called Mum "Baby". If she didn't eat her dinner, she got it for breakfast the next day. I did the shopping, so I know there was food in the house, but Patrona was intimidating, and she brought her own food, and I never had the nerve to ask what Mum ate.

Sometimes we took Mum to the farm, and sometimes to lunch parties or to the movies. She went down to Halifax for a couple of months during the next summer, Patrona was dismissed, and in the fall we hired Gina, a girl from the Philippines, who was connected to the women who looked after Dee and her sister. We were worried about Mum's mental state that fall, because she walked up to a perfect stranger and called him a jackass.

Gina was wonderful, a great friend and support for Mum. It was such a relief to feel confident that Mum was eating well, getting baths, and enjoying walks in her neighbourhood again.

I took Mum to lunch with some friends at the women's club "Twenty-One McGill Street" because our gay friend Dan had come back to Toronto and worked there as a waiter. Dan wasn't there that day, unfortunately, but Billy, the waiter we had, was charming. He said,

"Hi ladies, I am sorry there's no special today, so I guess the special is *me*" Without a pause, Mum replied,

"I'll have a piece of the loin then."

When Spiral Pottery folded, I took a job as shop manager for a local craft shop. My job didn't last long because it didn't make any money. On my days there I read, cleaned out my purse, took a writing course, wrote on a laptop computer, and one day I took my sewing machine into work and made a pair of pants. I was usually so busy that if a customer came in I resented the intrusion. One problem was that I was a sitting duck for loonies in the neighbourhood, one of whom was Hercules, and he came in almost every day. He had big widely spaced teeth, wild hair and beard, and he hadn't seen a mirror or a shower for eons. At first he just said that he was different from other men. Then he launched into a long explanation about the Greek Orthodox Church, visions he'd had, and the suggestion that he was the re-incarnation of Jesus. I guess that didn't amaze me enough, so he added that he might have been the Minotaur also, because of his huge sexual prowess. Studying the Greek Myths in grade nine, we learned that the seven maids and youths sent every year as tithe to the Minotaur were for his dinner!

Time stopped vanishing into the night after the craft store closed, and finally I could retreat into my basement studio to make pots again. It had been many months since I had been down there, and I had to squeeze past the obstacles which had accumulated over the winter: bikes, lawnmower, vacuum, flowerpots, kites, barbecue, lawn chairs, cases of empty beer bottles. One day there was a knock at the front door during the day when nobody was expected. It was a fellow who said he was the meter reader. He apologized for not having a badge to prove his identity, but since I found a two by four with some huge nails sticking out of it in the front hall, I let him in. The meter was in the basement, so I led him down past all of the obstacles, all the while keeping the lumber over my shoulder. To read the meter, he had to move some stuff that was leaning against the wall and he refused to do that. By some miracle, I got him out of there without any damage being done. The next day the genuine meter reader came, wearing a uniform and a badge.

I had sent out 20 invitations to lady friends inviting them to play hooky and come for lunch on Valentine's Day. A week before the proposed party, I was in the studio listening to Mozart, enjoying the freedom of my right brain, when the doorbell rang. Naturally I thought it was Bubba, the swarthy 300-pound rapist who had escaped from custody recently, probably impersonating a meter reader. I found a baseball bat among the paraphernalia on the stairs, and took it with me to answer the door, just in case. The front door had a window in it, I was delighted to find my old friend Linda, looking hopefully for lunch a week early.

Linda had been a friend of mine for 25 years, and when I first met her she was a brown rice moonchild. She told me all about yoga and astrology, Adele Davis, Maria Montessori, and Birkenstock sandals. She was one of the people who helped me shed my beauty queen persona and learn to love the integrity that comes from having clay and earth under my fingernails. The very strange thing was that she had completely reversed her direction, and was zooming into the void of high-pressure sales. She proselytized endlessly about the vast mountains of money she would create in her new business, marketing skin care products, in a pyramid scheme started by the Mormons in Salt Lake City.

The products were advertised as completely revolutionary, made out of chicken collagen and foetal cells – able to rejuvenate layers of skin. She was describing these fantastic products as though they would save the world from the Jihad, but I was watching her very carefully, and I could see that she had just as many wrinkles, eye bags, incipient wattles and dew laps as I had.

Wrinkles aren't the end of the road. My Uncle Byron staunchly believed that one shouldn't complain about getting older, because the alternative is so much worse. Besides that, I think I detect an infinitesimal increase in the respect and solicitude accorded me as I advance toward my dusty demise. After all, I am a grandmother: it is my duty to have age on my face.

The mention of foetal cells caught my interest though, because of a dream I had years ago about a cure for psoriasis, which had plagued my scalp for years. The dream was that I had to shave my head and make a poultice out of tiny foreskins of four different colours, all sewn together in little squares like a quilt. I had to collect the foreskins left over from circumcisions from hospital nurseries all over the city, and once the poultice was made of living cells, I had to put it on the shaved spot when I went to bed. In the morning, I ripped it off like a huge piece of tape, and then kept it in a very large Petri dish in a growth medium so it wouldn't dry out and die during the day.

Was this foreshadowing? Had I dreamed so many years ago about this miraculous new product? Wasn't this positive proof that I should take out a mortgage to buy a lifetime supply?

Linda had been on this bandwagon talking about nothing else for about 6 months; constant meetings and motivational sessions. Then she was taking seminars on business tactics, setting goals and ascending the ladder to money, power and control. She didn't listen to music anymore; she listened to tapes to keep her motivational levels topped up. She canceled her newspaper because it interfered with the process of realizing her goals. Her descriptions were breathless and overwhelming. Like the brainwashed, she had an answer for everything.

Utterly convinced that I would love to go to one of these seminars, she asked me earnestly about my personal goals. It was embarrassing to admit that my life is not goal oriented. I had a goal once, and even tried visualization to enhance the opportunity for its success. My goal was to run a pottery studio and make everybody successful and happy. I wanted to teach everyone in the universe to make pots. But then, we make plans and God laughs.

I accepted the fact that I wouldn't get anywhere with persistence, because although I had a well equipped pottery and lots of experience, I didn't have a master's degree in art, so the bigwigs wouldn't give me a grant. My philosophy had become "Ride the Horse in the direction in which it's going", and life was much less stressful.

I explained to Linda that I was a happy simpleton. In fact, I think the Spiral Pottery experience taught me that if I want something, I have to stop staring at it. Any teenager knows that staring at the telephone won't make it ring.

When I could squeeze a word in edgewise, I told Linda that if there were anything I wanted right then, it was a pair of roller blades, and the use of a strong dog for an hour three times a week. The dog would take me for a fast ride along the boardwalk beside Lake Ontario, so that I could feel the wind in my hair with out too much exertion. It almost seemed achievable too. Linda said,

"Maybe you have peace of mind then".

When Mark came home that evening, I told him about Linda's visit and our conversation. His reply was outrageous. He said that I am like Bart Simpson. This appeared to me to be an appalling insult, but then he told me about a dream he'd had in which he actually met Bart, who was a Spiritual Master. I guess Bart is a modern version of Alfred E. Newman, because his message was that we shouldn't buy into too much hyperbole about trying to be who somebody else wants us to be, rungs in the ladder, upward mobility, stress and heart attacks. It does take effort and single-mindedness to reject the constant barrage of advertising, to let go of what other people think. Be happy at the bottom!

Spain

In 1991, Mark and I went to Spain to visit with the Grotrians who lived next door to us in the country. They had a second house near Barcelona. At Mirabel Airport, we met some people in line who commented that Spain was a nice safe place, because Sadam Hussein kept two wives there.

Catalonia is a peaceful region of northeastern Spain on the "Costa Brava" where vacationers enjoy the Mediterranean, sailing, picnicking and swimming. The location is incredibly beautiful, with long wide sand beaches, rough red rocks and clusters of pine trees on top of steep red cliffs to the turquoise sea. Colorful fishing boats of every size and shape are pulled up on the beaches.

For the archaeologically inclined, there are remnants of civilizations that go back 2800 years, and the quaint medieval towns in the Pyrenees mountains still have the flavour of the middle ages. Busy local markets are found everywhere, teeming with fresh seafood, perfect fruit, vegetables and spices. As well, we devoured delicious chickens cooked on a vertical charcoal brazier right beside the road.

Because of its location linking Europe and Africa, Spain has been indelibly marked by many cultures. The earliest foreigners to settle there were Iberians and Celts, then Greeks, Romans, Visigoths, and Arabs. In about 500 B.C. the Greeks built a major city at Empurius on the Mediterranean coast. They minted coins and traded with other Mediterranean cities.

The Romans arrived in Spain in 218 BC, apparently to interrupt Hasdrubal from getting supplies to his brother Hannibal who was taking his elephants over the alps to attack Rome. The Roman occupation lasted six centuries, endowing future generations with the Latin language, Christianity and Roman Law. The Spanish Greeks were made Roman citizens and continued to enjoy the beautiful scenery and mild climate of Spain.

From partial reconstruction, it's obvious that the Greek city of Empurius was very grand, with markets, tall buildings with pillars, mosaic floors, wide avenues, and a huge hollow wall to fortify the town. The remains of lime kilns in the town indicate that an early kind of concrete was made to build the wall, about fifteen feet high, five feet wide and hundreds of yards long. The wall was built in the first century B.C. to ward off marauders. Lime was also used to make a plaster to line the cisterns that held drinking water underground. Two thousand years later, the ruins are overgrown with wild thyme, rosemary, english daisies and wild grape hyacinths.

Driving through the countryside in March was very soothing, the weather was warm, and wild plants were blooming everywhere, giving a wonderful fragrance to the air. Domestic almonds and magnolias were in flower and the hills were covered with potentilla and wild Iris. The leaves on the deciduous trees were starting to bud out, giving a lovely mauve and olive blush to the distance.

The towns of Camprodon and Besalu are perched high up in the Pyrenees. Both towns were built during Roman times and were visited by many crusaders on the way to and from England to the Holy Land. The towns had many beautiful arched bridges. Often the back of a medieval stone house was flush with a cliff, which dropped off several hundred feet to the rocky river bed below.

There's a wonderful outdoor market on a wide avenue with no cars. On Palm Sunday many of the stalls were selling palm fronds which had been twisted and braided into decorations to be used in religious ceremonies later in the day.

The Spanish people were relaxed and charming, and very well dressed. They closed their businesses for the afternoon, and opened up again in the evening. It seemed inefficient to sleep all afternoon, when the tourists need maps and stamps and necessities of life, but the Spanish didn't seem to have any particular notion of efficiency. They were very easy going, enjoyed life fully, and they were very nice to tourists. In Madrid we enjoyed watching businessmen drinking beer at breakfast to wash down their deep fried pastry. A shot of cognac in the coffee boosted them on their way through the day.

In Regencos, a tiny ancient town close to the seaside city of Bagur, the local restaurant had wine pumped into the basement every week the same way heating fuel is delivered in Canada. There is a free bottle of wine on every table, but water has to be bought. The town is carefully preserved by stonemasons who make alterations and extensions to old buildings that blend perfectly with the originals.

Spain has always been a favorite summer resort of the English and European people. Not only does it have a distinctive cuisine, wonderful scenery from mountains to oceans, it also has fabulous beaches and marinas. The spring is very pretty, and the fall is warm until November. The Mediterranean stays warm enough to swim in until very late in the fall. Most of the tourist population arrives in Spain in the summer months, from June to September.

La Bispal was the center of pottery making for the region. The pottery school was located in an ancient Franciscan monastery, which stood on a hill overlooking verdant fields, orchards, vineyards, red tile

roofs of the medieval town, and the snowy Pyrenees Mountains in the distance. In the garden of the monastery, the twelve stations of the cross were illustrated in ceramic tiles. The students learned traditional designs and techniques that go back to the sixteenth century.

With trepidation, we visited The Salvador Dali Museum in Figueres. We thought he was too weird, but the Museum was a delight as soon as we saw the outside. It is painted a rich dark red, covered with small concrete brioche, and it has giant white eggs on the roof. Inside, the paintings were extraordinary proof of his genius. One is a portrait of himself painting his wife between two mirrors. The scene repeats itself over and over. There's lots of silly stuff too, including gold möbius strips for bathtub faucets. Dali seemed to get bored easily with serious work, so he had fun creating absurdities. (We were glad to have missed the tumescent body bits and excrement.) His mustache was a source of great hilarity. Apparently he carried a jewel-studded cigarette case in which, instead of tobacco, he placed several mustaches, which he offered politely to his friends. Later we saw the castle he bought for his wife Gala with huge concrete elephants in the garden. The trees and hedges have grown up to make it a very private spooky little paradise.

Salvador Dali's Mustaches

Harmony

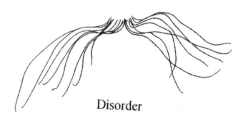

Disorder

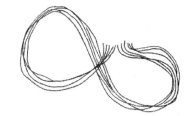

Möbius mustache

Splitting Hairs

Chapter Nine
Saint Mary the Vindicated

December 18 1990 was probably the fiftieth anniversary of my conception, since I was born September 18 1941. Mark's sons, Luke and Aaron, were with us for Christmas. On that evening, Aaron and his girlfriend Dena were eating cheese melted on English muffins instead of having dinner with us. They were talking about going to her house to study for her Math exam. Aaron was an ace at Math, so this was a good thing. I told them a joke about Mulroney and Bush.

Brian Mulroney went to Washington to see George Bush, who gave him a bit of advice. George said that to keep his boys on their toes, every morning he gave them a little puzzle. Along came Dan Quayle, and Mr. President stopped him.

"Dan, if your mother were pregnant, and the baby wasn't your brother or sister, who would it be? Dan thought for a moment, and said, "Sir, it would be me!"

"Very Good" said G.B.

Mulroney went back to Canada, and as soon as he saw Joe Clark, he asked the same skill-testing question. Joe was a bit baffled and walked around all day scratching his head. Finally Joe met Michael Wilson, and to the same question, "Who would the baby be", he answered correctly, "It would be me". Joe went back to Brian and said, "Well chief, I got the answer, it's Michael Wilson" and the Prime Minister replied, "No it isn't, dummy, it's Dan Quayle".

Because I told the joke, I know I was feeling friendly and funny, and not weirded out by teenagers, Christmas, or the fact that I would turn 50 in nine months.

Aaron and Dena went out, Donna, my star student and helper from Spiral Pottery, stayed for dinner with Luke, Mark and me. Donna showed us some wonderful slides of Costa Rica. After she left, I read my book Lilly, by Peter Feibleman, while Luke watched a basketball game with Mark, who took his usual evening snooze. At about eleven PM, I heard Aaron come in, and I realized, as he quietly went upstairs, that his girlfriend was with him. Slightly later, Mark and I went up to our attic bedroom to retire, and I noticed as we passed his room that Aaron's light was off. It made me think of my own dark girlhood gropings. Actually that's passive - I was the gropee. I mentioned to Mark that it probably was time to talk to his son about contraception, but he was too tired then. Tomorrow would be soon enough.

My book Lilly was the wonderfully funny and touching biography of Lillian Helman. Her personality was rather like my sister Annie's. Helman was a jealous, brilliant, bitchy, ornery hellion. She drank much too much and got away with it. Perhaps her biographer deserves the credit for making her look so wonderful, because he was in love with her and she was older than his mother.

152

Suddenly my book and the bed started to shake, and I calmly asked Mark if he thought we were having an earthquake. (Sound of snoring) He grunted negatively, he didn't think so, but I sure did. There was an earthquake here a few years ago and it felt just the same. A clay plaque hanging on the dresser rattled against the wood both times. I looked at the clock, just in case. It was 11:27pm. It seems to me that you won't know for sure until the next day, when you read about it in the paper, and they tell you the time it happened. A few minutes later, the house stopped shaking, so I knew that it really had been shaking.

About ten minutes after that, there was a knock on the bedroom door, and the quiet voice of Aaron calling his father. Mark woke up and went to speak in low mutters with him. Back in the bedroom, Mark said, " They were having sex, and the condom broke. I'm going to phone my boss if I can find his number" He wanted to phone his boss for advice because the guy was a doctor. Even so, I didn't think he would appreciate being called so late to be asked such a question.

Aaron took Dena home, and we had an excuse to go downstairs for another glass of wine and a smoke. We discussed this poor girl's mother, who thought that if Dena were visiting us, that she wouldn't get into trouble. We talked about how boys got too anxious and demanding, and girls just liked lots of petting. We wondered where kids got sexual information, and laughed about funny attitudes about sex left over from our Victorian parents. When he arrived home, I gave Aaron a copy of "Our Bodies Ourselves" which I found on the bookshelf. Its inscription said "To Sara, since you are now a young lady. I hope that if this book is too tame you will read it aloud to your little sisters, love, Paul".

There wasn't any point in giving Aaron hell, because he was a teenager, so we made jokes about my daughters, who were conceived to prove all of the statistics against coitus interruptus, diaphragms, and expensive German condoms. Then we started to laugh about the house shaking, and me being convinced that we had had an earthquake.

Aaron was a good student at Malvern and he played on the soccer team. In a dramatic save as the goalie, he ran to the corner of the goal, lifted his knee to protect himself, and the boy on the other team was running so fast that he impaled himself on Aaron's knee, detaching some of his internal rigging. Aaron went to see him in hospital, but there didn't seem to be anything to fear until we were served with a $250,000 lawsuit. The school had no insurance, but our house insurance company hired a lawyer and went to bat for us. After about two years, the insurance paid the family $25,000, and the problem was over. From day to day, he was a vortex for problems, including the house being infested with Scabies, accusations that he made obscene phone calls, and then he completely bombed on his final year of high school.

Aaron's hair was always a point of contention, and at that time, he was clipping off the sides, leaving the top about a foot long, and it was back-combed to mat against his head, with odd long antennae-like strands escaping from the nest. I would get into deep trouble when I asked him to brush it, accused of caring more about a person's appearance than about their soul, etcetera. After one such argument, I went over to Sara's for dinner, and as I walked in, I said, "Sometimes I think my house has been invaded by aliens!" and five year old Mathew looked up at his father and said,

"I just hate it when that happens, don't you Dad?"

154

Baffin Island

Gina took wonderful care of Mum and she wasn't the least intimidating. She knew how to give a sponge bath in bed, how to gently persuade Mum to get dressed, and to cook her favourite food. Mum went down to Halifax for the summer to visit with John and Cath, and Gina took the summer off, so I decided to go on a holiday myself, to paint in the Arctic. It was a good chance to find out if I had any talent, without anyone looking over my shoulder. If it seems peculiar to go to Baffin Island to learn to paint with water colours, let me say that it's wonderful not to have to tackle trees, flowers, barns, or waving grass. In the far north I didn't have to even think about mixing green, and sometimes the landscape turned off altogether, hiding behind a screen of thick fog. When the fog lifted though, the scenery was spectacular; snow capped mountains, glaciers and an eternity of sky .The sea is so many shades of blue, and seals are always popping up unexpectedly. "Awesome" takes on its real meaning in that environment.

We were a group of about twenty-five from across Canada and the United States, traveling with Trillium Workshops. Several members were professional painters and some just enjoyed painting as a hobby. Trillium's owner, Steve Szabo, took painters all over the world and he always seemed to put together compatible amusing people with lots in common. The wonderful thing about a painting trip is that you spend hours actually studying the landscape, and the feeling of the place sinks into your psyche as you struggle to give it justice on paper.

In Pangnirtung, we visited some native carvers who did their carving in packing cases, wooden boxes about four feet by four feet by ten long. The interior contained a chair and some power tools, piles of

155

raw soapstone that looked like rubble, and a lot of dust from the stone. The carver that we met was also a charismatic preacher. He churned out work at a fantastic rate, and gave all the proceeds to his church.

Since I had never painted before, I was the dunce of the class, and spent my time sketching and painting near our lodge instead of climbing mountains to paint spectacular vistas. Beautiful curious Inuit children came up and asked my name, my age, and if I had any children their age. A couple of girls pleaded with me to send them T - shirts and shoelaces from the teen group "New Kids on the Block" when I got back home. They looked through my sketchbook and squealed with delight when they found drawings of trees. One tiny girl named Daisy told me proudly that she had three children and four grandchildren. Since she was only about seven years old, I doubted her relationship with the truth. Her mother explained that Daisy had been named for a female elder of their town who had died just before Daisy's birth. The Inuit believe that with the name, the child inherits the soul, and even as a tiny baby, Daisy was treated with great respect by her former family. It was very nice to hear from this same woman that her children could be educated at schools in town, and they would not have to leave at eleven years of age to be educated in the south, as she had. Although she loved her Ottawa family very much, she said that it was difficult for a lot of young people to return to the Arctic after their years away. They lost the traditional way of life, and longed for the excitement of big cities.

The rocks of Baffin are wonderful to paint. They range from soft warm brown sandstone, carved into voluptuous shapes by the wind and sea, to cold, hard, sharp-toothed black granite. Some rocks, called "Erratics", are bigger than houses, and they perch precariously in odd places. Apparently, when the permafrost melts, huge bits of the mountain fall off. There are incredibly huge luminous blue-green icebergs floating in the sea, and miles of rolling tundra. Even though the landscape seems like the deserted barren bones of the earth, it is reassuring and peaceful in its simplicity. The tundra is beautiful in the fall. Tiny scarlet and yellow flowers contrast with black and white moss and lichen.

Cloud formations are fascinating too; sometimes they have flat white cirrus on top, sort of grey tweed in the middle, and puffy nimbus hiding the mountaintops. Fog seemed to be extruded on the surface of the water like a fat grey sausage, at about 20 mph. Then it would lift majestically and vanish. The silence was absolute. Sitting on a rock, I could hear the wings of the raven before I saw it fly overhead.

For lunch one day, we had spaghetti, which translates as "the rope that you eat" in Inuktitut. Afterwards we were visited by Amik, a wonderful native carver. The previous evening, this carver had sold a magnificent piece of sculpture to my roommate Jennie, and she was negotiating with him to go to his house to pay him for it. A younger native man was there at the same time, and after the first carver had left, he went up to Jennie, and said she should come to his house also. She wasn't sure what he wanted, and she declined politely. Then he got quite excited and said, "O.K. you come! Parents hunting!" She was appalled when she realized what his intentions were, because he was young enough to be her grandson. (Most Inuit are devout Christians, but that doesn't mean that they have lost their old ways of keeping warm. The Inuit are unfettered by our codes of behaviour.)

Jim, Alex, Jennie and I took a boat ride out into the Davis Straight to see if there were any whales. Amik was our boatman, and because the ignition switch was broken on his motor, he used his biggest screwdriver to complete the circuit. As he pulled the ripcord, a huge spark leapt out, which scared us half to death, but the engine caught eventually. He couldn't get an ignition switch in Pond Inlet; he

157

Waiting for the tide

would have had to buy a whole engine, so this method had to do. By his huge toothy smile, it was obvious that he loved the way it scared us.

His boat was very important to his life, he used it for fishing and hunting, and sometimes the hotel hired him to take tourists out. Amik's son Johnny was along for the ride, and the lady tourists always made a big fuss about him. He was only five, but he had his own hip waders. He hated to wear a life jacket because he felt he was too grown up. It didn't really matter anyway, he said, because if we sank, everyone would die fast in the freezing water.

Amik laughed at our funny " fat clothes." The Inuit wore only jeans and a warm shirt with no mitts in August, but we wore four or five layers on top and bottom, sometimes two pair of mitts and socks, plus woolly hats and scarves. We waddled like colourful penguins.

For future paintings, we photographed an iceburg as we approached it. Jim watched through binoculars for seals and whales, and Alex looked in his bird book because he had never seen a Fulmar before. He wrote in his notebook about where and when he had seen it. Amik laughed and said that he thought that was very strange. After all, we weren't going to eat it.

Sitting next to me was Jennie, and she looked so sad that Amik asked if she felt seasick. She didn't answer, but stared into the distance with stone eyes and she didn't seem to be in her body. Jennie had come to this desolate brink of the world to get away from the grief that had engulfed her family after the suicide death of her 24-year-old daughter Samantha. Jennie was not prepared for the isolation of Baffin Island, the silence, the hugeness of the sky and sea, which made people seem insignificant. The barren scenery intensified her grief. As we sped across the water, the pain of the salt water and ice pellets singing her face improved her mood somewhat.

"Physical pain is easier to bear than mental pain," she said. "I could cry and nobody would notice. I am so tired of these tears, but I can feel them dammed up like Aswan. Maybe the pain in my face will scare away the eels in my stomach! I wish I could just snap out of it."

Abruptly the boat stopped and glided up to another one. The drivers were calling to each other in Inuktitut.

"I hope there's nothing wrong with the boat!" Jim said,

"My God, did you see how he starts that thing? That huge spark goes right over the gas tank and there aren't even any life preservers!"

Amik laughed and lit up a cigarette.

"Once we go hunting for caribou and ran out of tobacco. We smoke my shirt! Taste terrible!" then he laughed like a maniac: coughing, spluttering, hooting and slapping his thigh

159

"Did you learn to hunt from your parents?" asked Jim.

"Sure," Amik replied. "Whole family go together. Sometimes children die of starvation, and sometimes parents die too. Then many children were living with us. There were no doctors, so lots of people die with no medicine. We move all the time trying to find food. I lost two sisters who starved to death. Then we move back to Iqualuit and both our parents died of T.B."

"Good Lord" groaned Jim, "Did you have any family left at all?"

Amik continued, staring out at the horizon. "I went to live with Keevok, an uncle. He kept me alive and gave me his old clothes to wear. When I was ten, I went caribou hunting with my cousin and uncles. We were walking. I lost my boot crossing the river and I had to make another one out of my parka, but when I returned to the others, they weren't waiting for me. A little while later I found two caribou. Then my uncle found me and he shot them. We carried both to the camp on our backs."

The women were silenced by the tale of such incredible hardship. They couldn't imagine always being so close to the edge of death. The strange thing was that Amik didn't seem very upset by the telling. He was quite matter-of-fact about it, and although it must have been forty years later, he was still just delighted that he found the two caribou before his uncle did.

"What happened when people died?" asked Jim.

" We had to leave them behind, but pretty soon a baby would be born and it would get the name of the person who died. So the person didn't really die because they were alive again as a baby."

"That's confusing," said Jim, his eyebrows knitting together.

"Oh no, the elders decide, and the baby has two families, the one it's born into, and the one it left. Everybody knows. Spirits can turn into other things too, like birds and fish".

"So death isn't the end to you?" Jim was obviously puzzled.

"Oh no, it's in the middle, like the horizon," replied Amik, pointing off across the water.

"Well, it does sound better to be a bird flying free in the air than a freezing and starving human," Jim concluded.

I was concerned watching Jennie's reaction to this conversation about death. I knew how depressed Jennie was, how difficult it was for her to fight off her desperate feelings of loss. "Jennie, are you feeling all right?" I asked.

"I'm OK, I was just thinking about how different their culture is from ours. Amik, is it true that you put your old people on an ice flow and send them off to freeze to death on the ocean?"

"We used to," replied Amik " Freezing to death not so bad, just like sleep, and we all come back; sometimes fish, little babies or birds," as he handed her a snow goose feather.

"Wow, that's a relief," Jennie said, "Samantha might come back as a bird - or my grandchild!"

"That's right" said Amik , "*never finished!*"

Walking around town was endlessly interesting. The roads were dirt tracks, unpaved because of the shifting perma-frost. Not many cars used the roads, just trucks delivering oil and water. The natives had three-wheeled all terrain vehicles. In the evening we often saw two people on the front and a dead seal tied to the back. Houses are unimaginative little prefabs sent by ship from the south, always with a big oil tank on the side. Poles for wires and lights are set in huge piles of rocks because it was always hard to dig holes. The lack of charm of the towns is made up for by the wonderful people and the landscape beyond the edge of town. We walked for miles and miles every day, along the beach and across the hills to watch the sunset at eleven at night. Women from our group felt free to go for long walks with their sketchbooks. We were thankful that it was not until the last day that the hotel owner warned us never to leave the confines of the town without a native man with a gun because of the danger of hungry polar bears.

yellow school bus

From Pangnirtung, we flew north to Pond Inlet in a plane that was sectioned off so that the front half was for passengers, but the back half held food and supplies. Pond Inlet was on the north shore of Baffin island, on Lancaster Sound, and across the water we could see a huge glacier on Bylot Island. The winter school bus was a "komatik", or sled, painted bright yellow with "School Bus" painted on the side. Sometimes we saw a group of Inuit in front of their houses, gnawing on the ribs of a raw seal. Their faces would be covered with blood, and mothers would cut a bit off on their curved Ulu knife, and pass it on the sharp blade over their shoulder to the baby. They were having a wonderful party, but it looked grisly to us. They keep caribou heads with antlers attached next to whole carcasses on the front porch, along with anything else they've caught recently. Often there is a chest freezer outside the house, which was used to store food after a couple of days of feasting. It was hard to get used to the fact that nothing decayed in that climate, so there was no reason to wrap it up or refrigerate it.

Sled dogs were individually chained to stakes driven into the permafrost, up and down a river bed; the largest pack numbered about 27, probably three teams of nine dogs. They howled forlornly at night, and generally were a pitiful sight. They were fed twice a week or so, and at that time were thrown a hunk of raw seal meat, which they fought over. The meat rolled in the sand, and became filthy and very unappetizing looking. We felt great sympathy for the dogs, but there was no room for bleeding hearts in the Arctic.

The day we arrived at Pond Inlet, a "sea lift" was occurring. A huge freighter loaded with pre-fabricated houses, an oil truck, a dump truck, several boats, and all the necessities for the community for a year, was berthed off shore. Cargo was shipped by planes every day when the weather permitted, but the sea lift brought big things, because there are no roads from town to town. For 48 hours the men worked with the snow-plough pulling a wagon to deliver all the houses to the building sites. The foundations for houses were sunk in August the previous year, by dumping fill around metal supports put into holes made with a heated auger. The fill froze solid during the winter, and became permafrost, which supported the house when it was constructed.

The men who drove the dump trucks and the tractors worked all night because the building season was so short that they had to work around the clock while they could. This feverish activity seemed contradictory, because time is a rather vague concept to the native people. They live from day to day, and because of their nomadic history, often will leave a job to catch dinner for the family.

On the way back to civilization, we visited the most wonderful church in Iqaluit, designed by architect Ron Thom. It was shaped like a round icehouse; inside, the decorations were native scenes hand stitched in felt. The cross at the altar was made of narwhal tusk, and the kneeling cushions were made of sealskin. At the front of the church, the railings were formed by komatiks or sleighs on their sides. There is a nativity scene painted on a wall, which shows the baby Jesus in an igloo, and the wise men dragging a seal for the baby.

Baffin was a bewitching adventure. The people were delightful, the scenery fantastic. The powerful mental image of the brilliant warm Inuit smiles set against the haunting stillness of their land will never fade.

Nativity Scene

Mum had become resentful of being taken to her house on Sunday nights, and said that she was being "given the boot" so I thought it would be a good idea for her to live with us. I decorated Ali's room with a carpet, her favourite chair, paintings she liked, and a bird feeder outside the window. She settled in quite quickly because Gina came every day during the week to take care of her. My studio was in the basement, so I could come up for lunch, and be there for any emergency.

One night we asked our neighbours for dinner. Bruce came in wearing a mask with a pair of glasses and the nose was a penis. Mum glanced up at him and with a perfectly straight face said,

"Well you're cock-eyed aren't you?"

We had meetings for the Beach Studio Tour at our house quite often, because it was easier than getting a babysitter for Mum. One night, Gillian Fishman came in and Mum thought she was Veronica Lake, the beautiful blonde actress from the twenties. Gillian played the part perfectly and Mum enjoyed the meeting immensely, holding hands with Gillian the whole time.

We took Mum to a local wine tasting party and she enjoyed it except for the huge spittoon in the middle of the table, which she found disgusting. (To avoid getting drunk, the other guests spat into the spittoon instead of swallowing, but we valiantly drank everything that was offered.)

Annie came from England in 1993 for 3 months to take over the job of selling Mum's house. While she was in Toronto, she rented a store room (which we didn't see until the day of Annie's funeral) where she put things she liked, including Mum's mink coats. She invited John and me to choose ten things each from Mum's house, and she kept all the rest. She wasn't quite successful though, because she put all Mum's silver into the bottom of a huge cardboard box in the basement of Mum's house. The box appeared to be full of old bedding ready for the garbage, but it was very heavy. Upon inspection I was pleased to find a nice collection of silver trays, which I had re-plated and gave to Mum's granddaughters.

We had a reception at home for a friend who got married at Christmas time, and one of the visitors was very taken with the porcelain dinner set we used. She sat right down to order an identical set from me. Mum came along to see what was going on, and said, "Those plates are terrible! They are square! Plates should be round, and look at this mug; it touches my nose when I drink out of it. That's so rude!"

The woman who was making the order said, "Well I like them because they are unique" and Mum, disgusted, went off to see what else was the matter with my party.

Once she came up to me in the house with a letter addressed to me. "Where's Mary? There's a letter for her." she said.

"*I'm Mary!*" I said, with conviction.

"I know you *think* you are, but the real Mary is young and beautiful".

Her doctor came to see her once a month for vitamin B shots, a Podiatrist came for her feet, a roving dentist came and said she had the worst gingivitis he had ever seen, and that she should go into hospital to have 6 teeth removed. A general anesthetic wasn't a good idea, so we went to my dentist who wasn't as alarmed, took out one tooth that was loose, and the rest of her teeth came out individually. She would hand me a big brown old molar like a gift. I should have made a necklace for her.

We went to a Christmas show, just north of Toronto. Jack was a very well known potter, but he was generally annoyed by the state of the world and the difficulty of making a living as an artist. As we came out of the building, I said. "Boy, he's rude! I can't imagine why he would be so rude to me, after all, I am in the same business".

"Well, what do you expect, he's *just* a potter" she said.

Around the same time, The Gardiner Museum of Ceramic Art "Girls" were invited to have Christmas dinner at George Gardiner's farm in Caledon East. We had a fabulous dinner, and afterwards he gave a little speech and said thank you to all of us for helping to put his Museum on the map, and he handed over a cheque for $15,000,000.00. He was worried that since the R.O.M. had closed the McLaughlan Planetarium, that they might do the same to his Ceramics Museum. Because of that gift, the Museum continues to be a major force in the world of clay artists. My brother John's comment was *"Who* would give fifteen million to a bunch of *potters!"*

Some days, Mum hardly got up at all, but other days she sat in a chair in her room looking at picture books. She became very ornery, threatening to bite or kill us if we tried to get her to do something she didn't want to, like go to the bathroom, or have her nails cut. Her personal daintiness was at a very low ebb, and her ability to communicate was far exceeded by my 3 year old grandson, Mikey.

Mum fell in her room and was in a lot of pain, so I called "Telehealth" for a doctor who would make a house call. He ordered us to put her in the hospital. She could stand, so she hadn't broken anything, but he insisted that she needed Xrays. We refused when he agreed that for a cracked rib there was nothing they could do anyway. He tried to kill her with codeine instead. She had never reacted to painkillers before, but suddenly we thought she had had a couple of strokes. She had spasms, sleep apnea, didn't eat or drink anything for days, and couldn't speak at all. She did recover, but she wouldn't surface if the barometric pressure were low. When it was very high, she was up all day long, but then one day she didn't wake up, because it was raining. I was expected to attend my grandson Mathew's baptism, and I hoped to take her with me, but I couldn't decide if she were alive or not. I phoned my friend Juliet to ask if she would like to come over for tea, and after a short conversation, she said, "You want me to come over there to see if your mother is still alive eh?"

Annie came to Canada for the last time in the fall of 1994, to stay with Mark and Mum and me until her house in Toronto was renovated. I finally discovered what she meant when she had frequently muttered darkly, "Blood is thicker than water." She had always maintained that if we weren't related, she wouldn't even know me, because I was just "pretty and nice" (and she was far superior, being a member of Mensa). If we hadn't been related, she wouldn't have been able to move in with us.

At first she thought she had Bell's Palsy, and her Chinese herbalist told her it was caused by a cold east wind, from driving the car with the window down. By the time she arrived in Canada, she had a diagnosis of a malignant tumour in the inter-pharyngeal space in her neck. It was wrapped around her carotid artery, and pressed on the nerves that fed her face. She arrived with 2 quarts of liquid morphine, which she swallowed, by the spoonful. This was British medication, her doctors told her not to worry about becoming addicted to it because she was "morphine deprived". They didn't add that it was a medication for terminal cases. Annie lived with us in our house for three months because she was too sick to be alone. Mum was in an electric hospital bed because she had hurt her back, and when she saw Annie in the hall, she would grumble,

"Who *is* that little witch?" and Annie would complain, "I don't know why you take care of *her*. I am *way* sicker than she is."

I had to take Annie to various appointments, and one of them was to see an MD at a local clinic. He was asked to supply morphine, and when he heard how much Annie took, he said, "Holy Shit!" He acted as though he thought we were suspicious dope addicts and pushers, but he did eventually write her a prescription for pills.

Another appointment was with a dentist who was removing her mercury fillings. He diagnosed "Thrush" and gave her a prescription for a vaginal suppository which women use for yeast infection, but he told her to put it in her mouth. The pharmacist couldn't believe the prescription, and had to phone the dentist for confirmation while we waited, red – faced.

Another health practitioner told Annie she had a nest of parasites living in her neck, and she needed wormwood to kill them off. The "thing" was getting pretty big, and eventually she couldn't swallow anything but grapes. She was in complete denial, and with the wormwood and the grapes, she was sure she would win, in spite of what her doctors said. She always had a scapegoat, and for her illness, she blamed her orthodontist because he moved her teeth too aggressively when she was a teenager, she blamed Bob for not painting her bedroom, and she blamed Mum for not giving her a packet of self-esteem when she was a kid.

Mark and I found an acupuncture machine on the market, which claimed to alleviate pain. We bought her one, took her for an appointment to learn how to use it, and went to the farm for the weekend. Her English doctors had told her not to worry about getting addicted to morphine, so she stopped taking it suddenly, believing that the acupuncture machine would take care of her pain. By three in the morning, her levels had worn out, she started screaming in her bedroom, and we rushed in to help. She was in agony, and commanded that I kill her with a kitchen knife, right then and there. Somehow in the high drama of the moment, I had the wits to remember that she had left some morphine pills at the farm the previous weekend, so I was able to find them and get some relief for her. She was so exhausted that she didn't get up the next day.

Finally her house was finished and the bill was higher than she expected because she calculated the work at forty hours a week, when it was actually about sixty to finish in time for Christmas. I had gratefully paid the contractor the full amount, and not only did she refuse to reimburse me, she called me an idiot for being "taken" by him. I was very relieved when Bob arrived from England and they finally moved into her house. It was obvious to us that this would be her last Christmas, so we all went to Mum's weekend farm, and ineffectively tried to be nice. The niceness deteriorated at the table when Annie asked to say grace before we ate, and Mark accused her of being a hypocrite for going back to Christianity in the last few months of her life. Mum went into her room and slammed the door. Bob told Annie that she was blackmailing us with her illness, and they raged on until they ran out of booze.

Dear Aunt Gracie died on Christmas Eve. We lost our beautiful island at Lake of the Woods that fall also. The island was owned in eight shares by the family, but our Aunt Beth decided that people from "the east" couldn't look after it properly so she promised it to her Winnipeg friends who had been renting it for years. I refused to sign away Mum's share because every time the subject came up, she growled, "Over my dead body." Annie said she would sue me if I signed. Aunt Beth threatened to disown us, and Gracie's lawyer phoned up and accused me of hastening her death by not signing. I was the last holdout but I finally caved.

By New Year's, Annie was in hospital having a gastric tube inserted so she didn't have to swallow anymore; she could put nutritional liquid directly into her stomach. I also saw her pour straight gin down the tube. She was still painting and she enjoyed her house until March when she had a stroke and died two days later.

The funeral was like a Fellini movie, it was on a blustery April Fool's Day for one thing. I stood at the front of the church and sang so lustily that the Minister invited me to join his choir. The casket was made of cheap unfinished plywood, and when it was placed in the ground, Bob fell on his knees, and cried, "Oh Annie, I am so sorry, I forgot to bring you anything, so here are some subway tokens," as he threw them on the casket. A long passage from the Bible about "Hear us Lord, groaning and grutching" was dramatically read by Annie's son John. Mum was horrified, and decided she had to leave the minute she saw the hole in the ground for the casket. Mark drove her home, convinced that she believed that the grave was for her.

The reception was in the basement hall of a church in Regent's Park, a run down neighbourhood of Toronto. The Minister said that we should not drink wine because there would be lunch for indigents in the basement at the same time, and wine might cause a furor. It was a location of extreme grunginess, with no catering service, but people left after a short time, and no rubby-dubs raided us, even though we drank quite a bit of wine. After the funeral and the reception, we went back to Annie's house, where Bob read the will, which cut her children off with a rebuke, and left everything to Bob, who immediately blamed me for cutting off her kids. He told them, "This is obviously Mary's doing, because she drove Annie to the lawyers."

In fact the first lawyer I took her to wouldn't write the will for her, she had to go to an old University friend to get what she wanted. Another scapegoat for Annie was having had enough income to survive without working, and she blamed that for not having become a famous painter.

Chapter Ten
Cowering from Cows

In September 1997, my daughter Beth bloomed like a lotus, was married and assimilated into a rather large male bastion called Kilcoo Camp. Many people asked me how had she become this poised confident woman, when we all remembered her as shy, fearful and withdrawn as a child. She made a wonderful speech extolling the virtues of her sisters and family and her new husband, whom she obviously adored. Her new family was hearty, backslapping, hockey loving, Conservative voting, Anglican Canadian. They thought I was a cute artiste.

The weekend started on Thursday with the rehearsal dinner, all very nice except that it gave me Kaopectate disease for Friday. It's hard to tell if you've et something bad or if you have the flu, so I avoided people for the day, but it passed, and having had nothing to eat or drink for 24 hours, I was ready to eat, drink, and rock and roll by party time.

It was a dour day with a brisk wind and scudding clouds, rain in the morning, fall colours beginning to happen, and about 45 minutes of sun, right at the time of the wedding. Beth came to the rocky promontory "Chapel Point", standing up in a boat, wearing the hunting tartan over her gown. Her father Tom stood beside her in his kilt, the bagpipes played "Mara's Wedding", the wind blew her veil straight out behind them. It was a great sight! The wedding was short and well rehearsed, but the Reverend dropped the ring with the diamonds in it just as things were getting underway. The surface they were standing on was a dock-like structure with wide spaces between the boards, and no carpet. The ring was safely retrieved, but the Rev. declared that the best man had dropped it. Afterwards I reproved him, since I had a perfect view of the proceedings from the front row, I knew that he had, in fact, dropped the ring. He gave me a fierce look and said,

"Who would ever believe you. I am a man of **God!**"

The speech by the father of the bride was wonderful; he spoke of her ability to meet challenges, her skiing prowess and bungee jumping in New Zealand. She survived an attack by a bear while tree planting. It made us all shed a tear or two. After the speech, I spoke to his brother who said, "I used to think he was such a jerk, do we have to be nice to him now?"

At one point in the evening, the best man invited the Rev to join him at the lectern, and when the two of them were eye to eye, he presented a gold edged tome that looked like a Bible and said,

"Put your hand on this Rev, and tell me you didn't drop the ring" The Rev snatched it away and retorted,

"This is the *Book of Common Prayer!*" and retreated to his seat.

After the speeches, there was a huge display of fireworks, then dancing. The band was fabulous – they played Elvis, Be Bop a Lula, Sh Boom, Don't be Cruel, Rock around the Clock all our favourite tunes from the fifties. Fabulous dancing continued for a couple of hours. We stayed in a hotel in Minden over night and Mark's last words concerning Beth's wedding to Kilcoo Camp were from Star Trek.

"Resistance is futile, you will be assimilated."

On Sunday, there was a service at Chapel Point. It reminded me of the Sermon on the Mount in its simplicity. The Rev. wore jeans and a sweatshirt with the ecclesiastical stole around his neck, so it was quite informal. The worshippers had hang-overs-on-the-rocks. The Rev. had a bun and a glass of wine for communion. Five dogs joined us, all trying to get the bun, swimming in the lake, and shaking all over the Rev. It was hilarious, and he told some great stories about his career, as it had been his ordination 32 years previously, on St. Matthews Day. At the end he mentioned that he had known the groom's family for 30 years, and he would never forget this wonderful wedding because indeed, he *had* dropped the ring.

In 1998, I bought a lovely new Subaru, named Kevina, after Kevin, a beetle we once found at the farm, who was the same marvelous iridescent green. My only concern about my new car was its automatic windows and doors, but there was nothing I could do about it. I had to learn to use them, and remember that people sitting in the car with the ignition off could roast to death on a hot day. I had been driving my mother's ten-year-old Volvo since she had come to live with us. It had 2 doors, and the back windows didn't open at all, simplicity itself; sadly unappreciated by me until too late.

Sara went to Berlin for a conjugal visit with her husband who was making a series of TV programs, and the children were distributed among their three grandparent units. I had Mikey, and the dog, Charlie, who was as big as a small moose and about as well trained. His worst quality early on seemed to be stinkiness – both B.O. and gas. Mikey's car seat was properly installed in the back seat of my new car and Charlie was on the floor beneath his feet. Twice during the ride to my house, Mikey opened the back door, so I had to stop and read the instruction book about the kid locks, which were easy once you knew where the buttons were. He had fun making the window go up and down with the magic button. I had to park on the street instead of in the garage so I could get Mikey out of the car seat, and as I struggled to unhitch him, the dog bolted through my legs and went charging up the street. The only voice he responded to was in Berlin, so I locked Mikey in the car and went after the dog. We had two bunnies in 1982, and when they escaped from their cage one early morning, Ali went after them screaming invective, but Beth took a lettuce leaf out of the fridge and coaxed the bunnies back with a loving friendly voice. It doesn't work with dogs. Charlie finally found something irresistible to sniff and I stamped on his leash. Then I had to get Mikey, who was hysterically wiping away his tears and hiccupping. I had to carry his forty pounds across the street and up the 20 stairs to the house with Charlie and gravity both trying to kill us at the same time. I kicked the dog as hard as I could with excellent results. By this time I didn't even notice his bad smell.

Waiting for us in the house was my ancient mother, who took a dim view of disorder and entropy, which we embodied to perfection. She would prefer to look at photographs of her great-grandchildren than actually see them. We received a frosty reception. Even though she seemed to be completely senile, she was still in command of her opinions and the disapproving look. She retaliated by dropping a big steaming turd on the floor on Easter morning. (Her warning system wasn't very good.)

Mikey was 18 months or so, and he was terribly entertaining. He didn't need toys because he invented things to do as he went along. Lots of puzzles engaged his attention, like how to get a piece of Lego onto a protruding nail. He figured things out by focusing on them until they were undone. Then he went on to something else, maybe something like a piece of fluff that would jump up in the air when he punched the bed. He was very amusing, and loved to dance.

Mikey slept like an angel for 12 hours. In the morning I had to wait outside his door to see if I could hear him because he would just lie there peacefully with his eyes open. Charlie the dog wandered around all night, clicking his toenails on the floor and heaving sighs and rolling over lumpily.

On Good Friday, we went to the park with swings and slides and other little kids. Mikey disliked swings, but loved the slide. He insisted on climbing up the slide instead of going around to the stairs. Sara's kids didn't respond very well to the word NO, so I tried to encourage him to get in the line with the other kids, but he wasn't interested. I wasn't sure about playground etiquette in the nineties, so I just had to hope for the best. It worked, nobody got smeared and no irate father tried to arrest me. Mikey did get to go down the slide a lot more often than everyone else. We stayed for two hours, and he was so exhausted that he was willing to go home for lunch and a nap.

Ali and her girl friend Erin came over later that day to help with family minding, and brought their dog Sacha who also had long toenails. Charlie and Sacha ran around, jumped up on people and lay in awkward places like doorways, and right in front of chairs. They

179

barked like maniacs and freaked the cat out so badly that he hid upstairs for hours, and when he appeared he bit Mikey in the face. Then Charlie peed on the rug. Not just once, but three times, three different rugs. He watched me balefully as he did it – I guess he could tell by my face…or was I screaming? Mark and the girls took pity on him, so he was taken out to run around at the park, and then they took him for a bath on Saturday because his smell bothered other people too.

Don't think we hate dogs! Mark and I have a lovely Border Collie named Percy who is perfectly obedient and smells like sandal-wood, but he is figmentary, and somewhere in the future.

Mikey loved nothing better than to dance, his favourite music was M BOP by Hanson – I didn't have it, but we had a lovely time dancing to the Beach Boys. I taught him the twist and the mashed potato. He danced like a wild man jumping and clapping and spinning around. He responded to music very enthusiastically if it had a beat. Maybe we should have changed his name to Michael Flateley – he looks rather Irish, thick black hair and bright blue eyes.

On Sunday we went to the Easter Parade and saw three elephants at the end of our street. He was not impressed, the Easter candy was gone, so back at the house he amused himself by stealing Mum's bib which is made of flannelette, just like his favourite blanket. Mum was pretty bent over by then, and she ran after him exclaiming, "That boy needs a spanking!!" and then she fell trying to smack him.

I thought it was time to take him home, so we got ourselves together, I put him in the front seat of the car, he happily climbed into the car seat in the back, and I backed the car out of the garage. I had to strap him into his seat, so I stopped the car on the sidewalk and walked around to the back door. He had locked the doors as I walked around, so I stuck my head through the half open window to see if I could reach in and open it from the inside, and Michael pressed the window button, and rolled the window up on my neck. Wow did that hurt!! It didn't seem to want to stop, so I was lucky that my arm was inside the car through the window, and I could reach the button to roll the window down again.

The first time I went to La Jolla was in 1968, for Grandfather Gourley's ninetieth birthday in February, and in 1998 three-year-old Mikey came to visit me there with Sara, in the same apartment at The Beach and Tennis Club. He loved the beach, the birds and the sun. My Aunt Beth was very entertained by him. Her memory was shot, and I think her doctors must have been insane. One day I asked if she would like to go for a walk, and she said that she had to lie down because she had cramps. Apparently her doctor had put her on the birth control patch so she wouldn't get osteoporosis, and at ninety, she was having menstrual periods.

My daughter Beth was having a very exciting life. She went on "safari" in Kenya over the March break with some kids from Kilcoo Camp, and then she and David went to South America, Rio and Buenos Aires to tutor the children for the road manager for the Rolling Stones while they were on tour with Mick Jagger! The road manager's kids went to Kilcoo Camp too. I didn't see much of her, she was working for the camp a couple of days a week, spent 3 volunteering as an art therapist at Regent Park School, and weekends were at camp.

At 5 A.M. one morning in 1994, we heard Mum fall in her room. She was lying on the floor, and since it was five in the morning, we lifted her onto the bed, and then phoned the doctor. She called us back at about ten, and said that if Mum's legs were different lengths, she had broken her hip, and we should call an ambulance. The stretcher had to go down a flight of stairs in the house which had a tight angle, and then the sixteen stairs at the front of the house, which were also treacherous, but Mum was tied in tightly, and even when the stretcher had to be lifted up so that it was almost vertical, she didn't seem to be afraid at all. She was operated on the next day, but she never learned to walk again. After the hospital had done what it could, she was moved to Providence Villa, where she had three roommates who were in worse shape mentally than she was. Gina continued to visit Mum every day, and as long as she was there, everything went very well. Gina would take her to watch the birds at a bird feeder, and just being out in the hall watching the other people was entertaining. Ali and I went on weekends and days when Gina couldn't make it. It was a depressing building, and we thought that there must be a more cheerful facility in the city. We found True Davidson Acres, which was more modern, had smaller rooms, and they also had several resident cats that purred in the laps of the inmates. I was in a pottery show in downtown Toronto one day, and phoned the nurses station at Providence Villa to see how things were going. The nurse said,

"Fine, I think...but wait a minute, there's your daughter Ali wheeling her down the hall. Your mother has her coat on, and her suitcase is in her lap!"

Ali had reserved a room at True Davidson home, which was more to our liking, and since Providence Villa wasn't fast enough to release Mum so that she could get to her new room before dinner, Ali decided to kidnap her.

Mum was in a wheelchair because learning to walk after hip surgery was too difficult, and at the new home the chair supplied had no tray in the front and no lap belt. This was because a lap belt was considered to be a "restraining device". The problem was that a nurse would wheel her into her room, then leave to get help to move her into bed. While the nurse was gone, Mum would make a lunge for the bed and fall on the tile floor. One time she was dropped from a sling. She had refused to get up, but the rules said she had to get up, so they had her lifted out of bed by machine. She was furious, and struggled so violently that she landed on the floor. The head nurse had to phone me up and say, "We have had an incident..." I guess the worst was the day that a nurse's aid tried to get Mum out of bed by leaning over her, pulling on her opposite shoulder. Mum bit her so hard that she drew blood. They had to learn not to mess with Helen. We were threatened with her being isolated with the badly behaved and extremely difficult patients. She died before that happened though. It was after lunch; Gina was helping her into bed for her nap, when she grabbed her chest in pain. She was sent by ambulance to The Toronto East General Hospital. I was teaching in the "Feats of Clay" program at the Gardiner Museum of Ceramic Art that day, and the phones weren't working. While I cleaned off the tables at the end of the class, finally the phones were fixed, and it was a call from Ali, to say that I should go directly to the hospital. In the emergency department, Mum was hooked up to monitors, which slowed down and stopped over a period of about an hour. Then the doctor came into the cubicle and said that I should leave because they didn't like dead people in Emergency. There was another room for me to sit in; maybe I should make a phone call.

The funeral was not difficult because I had contacted "The Simple Alternative", which made arrangements before the event. Mark's father, Alan, had been a preacher, so it seemed appropriate for him to give the main address. Just before we printed the order of service, Sara let me know that she wanted to say something, so I slotted her in after Luke.

Luke had written a song for Helen because he lived with us for a couple of years before she died, and he and his girlfriend Ruth had taken care of Mum on many weekends when we went to the farm. Poor Sara was in tears after Luke sang his song, and she could hardly speak. Here are the lyrics to "Grandmother Child" © Luke Koleszar-Green.

There she sits in her chair on her own

Passing time, waiting to go home,

I wonder what she used to be like before

I wonder if she even knows anymore

Her child-like eyes are looking at me

With innocence and tranquility

It won't be long now, of that you can be sure,

And when you go I won't forget you.

Now she's talking to that empty chair

"How do you do, how long have you been there?

You're always welcome around here don't you know,

There's a bed for you upstairs, so don't you go."

184

She sings along with me as I play my guitar

She's out of tune

But I like her singing anyway

It makes her happy she says.

You don't know what you meant to me

You don't even know my name,

You don't know what you've given me

But thank you just the same

You're on your way to Heaven soon I know

My journey's just begun

I might see you somewhere down the line

When I've done all my time.

Thank you for your humour and your dignity

Thank you for your time

Thank you for showing me

That life's not such a bitch all the time.

Having been urbanites for 55 years, Mark and I moved to Mum's country property after she died. Our telephone listing in the phone book was for H. Lazier, and one day a man phoned up and asked to speak to her. I said that unfortunately, she had passed away. "Fine" he said, " I will cancel the phone right away."

"Wait a minute!" I said, "I am her daughter and I pay the bill, so please don't cancel the phone service." He said, "Dead people can't have phone numbers." and I replied, "Well, I pay the bill every month, and I need a phone." and he scolded, "You should have changed your name in the phone book." My reply was " I knew that you would charge me a hundred dollars to change the H to an M, so I didn't bother".

"May I please speak to your supervisor?" Mark came into the conversation after having heard the beginning from his phone in the studio. A long harangue ensued, and the supervisor agreed to change the initial to M from H in the listing, and now the bill comes to Mark Lazier, to prove that people who don't exist can have phone numbers, just not the deceased.

To meet people and become part of the community, we joined a couple of studio tours and suddenly we knew about fifty artists. Friends came up from the city, and eventually we got to know some neighbours. One weekend two friends came up, Judy and Anne, and because it was so hot, we decided to go over to the Dufferin County Museum to enjoy the air conditioning. The Museum was hosting a final drama exam for one of the local high schools, and we were told that we could go down to the basement to see the collection of artifacts. They even let us into the inner sanctum where the public isn't allowed. In this specially air controlled room, there are shelving units which move on tracks. At the end of a shelving unit, there is a wheel that moves the unit. We had to wear white gloves to use the wheel, and as it turned, the unit moved along the track to expose the next set of artifacts lying on the shelves. I enjoyed moving the wheel so much that Anne wanted to try, but she found it much harder. The unit seemed to be stuck, and then a lady jumped out and said, "You are squishing my husband!" When he appeared, he said that he had been preparing to jump onto one of the shelves if he were squished any harder. After that, the three of us witnessed a woman who was donating her grandmother's wedding undergarments to the Museum. They were amazingly unimaginably large. Another fit of giggles overcame us and we had to hide in the elevator so nobody would hear us.

Our new country life sounded bucolic: sweet endless weekends, heathery tweeds, Constable paintings from every window and fields of blowing wheat.

Here's why I never had a dog. Dogs have a sad lack of couth, bad halitosis, they gobble their dinner, and then pass gas from every orifice all night.

Abner, a black Lab, belonged to our neighbors, he slept with his eyes unnervingly open and he urinated on my garden right in front of me!

His owners, Sara and Christian, had to go to England to rescue some elderly lady relatives from each other. Christian's autistic cousin was born in a shelter during the Blitz, and she was being cared for by his overbearing, cantankerous mother Elizabeth, who at 92 was very fond of whiskey. They had to straighten things out in England, leaving us to look after their small herd of black Angus, about 25 cats, and Abner.

We had to have lessons about feeding the cows. They liked lots of hay, and grain every two days; be *very* careful to cut off all the string that wraps the hay bales or the cows can choke to death. I was telling this story to a friend in the city and she said,

"What!! Don't they have grass up there where you live?"

Mark drove the tractor with a spike on the front over to where the big round bales were stacked, and carefully boinked one right in

187

the middle. Then he drove with it perched on the spike over to a big metal feeder in the middle of the muck in the barnyard. Even the tractor felt ornery trying to drive through it. The hay bales were tied up with miles of binder-twine, and we needed to cut it off quickly, because as soon as the cows realized that we were in the barnyard, they started to accumulate to get munching as fast as they could. The barnyard was deep in mucky manure; it was easy to drop the knife as it was cold and we were wearing gloves, I had to find the twine and cut it, pull off great lengths of it, not drop it, and keep an eye on the great lumbering beasts (slowed somewhat by being up to their knees in gooey muck). I obviously have spent too much of my life worried about whether or not I look good doing whatever I'm doing, instead of whether or not I can move fast and not fall down or drop anything in 2 feet of wet manure.

Our instructions were to give them grain every two or three days. The grain came in heavy bags tied up with string, which we transfered into buckets, and then it went into the feeding troughs in the barn. There wasn't space in the barn for all the cows, and the calves didn't even get into the barn for a taste. I always thought that cows would spend the winter inside the barn, but this barn isn't big enough. Do the poor things just totter around on the snow and ice with huge drifts on them? The cows became very upset and gave us a good bawling out if they came all the way down from the pasture through the muck into the barn to find us only feeding the cats, not putting out grain for them.

There was also a bull. He was not much bigger than the cows, and hard to recognize and avoid for that reason. Sometimes he gave me a sideways glance and stuck out his big lipstick. That's when I jumped over the fence and sent Abner after him. This was Abner's forte: he barked and chased the bull while I cowered in the bushes. Cowering from cows!

In spite of Henry David Thoreau's admonition to " beware of new undertakings which require new wardrobes", we had special outfits for the barnyard. Everything was smooth so the hay didn't stick. No red because of the bull. We needed pockets on the outside, old gloves, boots with socks. Two pair of socks is best. Mark's boot was sucked into the muck, he pulled out his foot, barely maintained his balance by putting his sock-clad foot down in the muck. The sock went over the fence and the bare foot went back into the boot. We learned everything the hard way. We had a problem with where to keep the boots. Manure smells just as bad in the car as in the house, so outside seems best, but rain and dead mice ended up inside the boots and that's disgusting! A Scottish "Wellie Rack" is the thing we needed, vertical dowels attached to the porch on which one upends the boots; still cold, but dry and no dead mice inside them.

One Saturday we went down to do our chores and the naughty cows had pulled down the electric fence, which was there to protect the big hay bales from destruction. They stomped on the wire, and were happily eating their winter supply of food. We arrived with Abner who leaped out of the car barking, shooed them away. I hate to see the cows run though, what if one fell in a gopher hole and broke her leg? They might never ask us to look after their cattle again!

Have you ever heard the joke "Why doesn't a woman over fifty have babies?"

"Because she would put the kid down somewhere and forget where she left it!" Well it's absolutely true. I had to look after my 3 grandchildren, aged 3, 7 and 11 for two weeks, and I couldn't remember who hates butter, or tomatoes, how to buy enough snack food, who drinks milk, when to admit that I can barely figure out grade two Math, let alone grade six. Mathew had a question in his Math homework, which asked for a rectangular shape in which the perimeter was to be 36 and the area was to be as small as possible. We even phoned Mark the mathematician and he couldn't answer it. Mia's question was called a Math Sentence, written like a fraction: eight over part, plus six over part, equals fourteen over sum. But it's not a fraction because the denominators are different, and it's not a sentence either!

There was also good old Charlie the dog; he should have been bald because of all the hair he shed. I swept like Fantasia and still it swirled in little black clouds. The dog smelled bad, having been recently sprayed by a skunk, but it was the clanking of his toenails that really drove me crazy. He got up and flumped around, clanking his toenails about every 2 hours all night long.

Taking a walk with Charlie was quite an event. He had never been trained to a leash, so when we put one on, he ran around the kids and me (herding us, just doing his job as he sees it) so we were all tied up in the rope. Better than that was when he tangled it around his own back legs and hobbled himself. That way he couldn't lunge at other dogs, and he had to hop along with 3 legs at a more moderate speed - much better for my arm holding Mia's hand and the leash. The neighbours must have thought I was a sadistic fiend!

Then there was Nina, the Italian lady next door, who phoned twice a day to see if the kids were still alive. If I were stupid enough to answer the phone before looking at the display to see who was calling, she said rudely,

"Who IS this?" I meekly told her it was Sara's mother.

"You sound too young!" she said accusingly.

I mentioned to her that Tom's mother had died and there was a nice funeral. "Nice?" she frowned, "What's nice about a funeral!"

"Oh well", I said, "The music was lovely and Tom made a very nice speech, we were celebrating her life... You know."

"I don't believe in that!" she said, "Funerals should be religious!"

At his mother's funeral, Tom credited his mother for being a genius at laundry. I wished I could speak to her about my laundry nightmare at Sara's house - how to appease the God of odd socks. I had an impressive pile of them, which grew in height and girth everyday - like a very large amoeba, it was taking over the bedroom. When Mathew needed socks in the morning he went to the pile, and if he were lucky he came out with a pair that matched. This pile was huge when I took over the housekeeping, and it may have groan a bit under my reign, but only because I swept under the beds.

I have to admit that I've become a health food nut over the past thirty years, so making lists, shopping, reading labels, baking granola, steaming vegetables and eating fish has all become part of my persona. I had to add to this: wait for 15 minutes while the kids stare balefully at dinner and then throw it all in the garbage to complete the cycle. One night I made macaroni and cheese from real cheese, and Mikey had a complete meltdown, screaming as though he were being murdered. I had put a bit of thyme in it and he found it to be *very* offensive. Then it was Fettuccini Alfredo and Spinach - three servings directly into the garbage. Mikey liked "Frankenfood". Corn Pops, plastic cheese ropes, cheese slices, chips, and chocolate and coke for breakfast. For dinner he often had corn pops with "goldfish" on top. Some days he ate nothing, and some days he ate non-stop.

Mathew stomped on a drinking box one day and we discovered that the inside was lined with shiny metal foil- could this be aluminum? Were they getting Alzheimer's early? I wondered this often because of the wonderful confabulations they came up with. One night I hired a babysitter and went out to see a friend, and when I came home, Mathew was still up, furious at Mia for putting soap on his dental retainer. He couldn't wear it to bed because it was ruined, so I told him about purification by baking soda, and that usually people keep it in the refrigerator (important life lessons here). The next morning he couldn't go to school because he had such a stomachache from the soap on his retainer (purely imaginary according to Amelia). I informed him that I have a B.S. detector, which he thought was such a good idea that he accused Mia of B.S. every time she opened her mouth. Mathew's report card wasn't very good, but he said it would improve because his father was going to give him an ATV if he got higher marks, the week after that it was a Porsche! Mia told me that a mean teacher killed her guinea pig by spraying Windex on it, and also that on midnight of the new millennium, all the Beanie Baby factories were going to blow up. For Halloween, Mia dressed up as a scary witch with a wig, a pointed hat, and she painted green warts on her face. We were having supper before they went out to trick or treat and Mathew came to sit at the table. He said, with the utmost scorn,

"God Mia, your warts are symmetrical!"

On the weekends we drove to the farm where Mark was glad to see us and the scenery was new and interesting. Mathew, Mia and Charlie went to their Grand-dad Tom's for part of the time, during which we noticed that Mikey didn't scream or whine even once. We had fun in the pottery making Christmas presents; they were all very well behaved during the Saturday morning pottery class. Upon looking over the eastern vista at the black Angus grazing in the next field, Mia exclaimed,

"Holy Crud!"

and Mikey said,

"Are your cows on remote control Granny?"

Even though I swore off having a life for two weeks, I was very active and exotic in a vicarious way. We received phone calls from Namibia almost every day, where Sara and Andy were having a great holiday, buying jewels and snow boarding on sand dunes of all things. I hoped to be far *far* away when the phone bill came, having watched Mat mumble through long conversations while playing a computer game at the same time - long silences, no news, just trying to keep the line for himself, not give it up to the other kids.

My stepson Aaron was on the front of TIME magazine that week, getting his head stomped and his arm bent out of shape by the police in the Seattle riots. He was a career radical and traveled across Canada by train to pick up other protesters. The whole thing was fueled by e-mail, and it looked as though they made people listen to their protest against the World Trade Organization. The arrested protesters were put on a bus, which they refused to leave for four days. They had no food and the bathroom area was a designated spot at the back of the bus. Finally the police used tear gas to get them out.

We had a letter from Russia all beautifully hand written in Cyrillic. The only part of it that we could understand was on the back, the names and addresses of 3 banks, including American Express. We are getting used to seeing people begging on the streets of Toronto, but this is very sophisticated international begging. Mark once sent a hint to a gardening magazine, which included our address, and we have had three people correspond with us since then. The hint was that male urination around the garden keeps away animal pests.

Most exotic of all was a letter from the "Tasman Challenge", a freighter steaming from Jakarta to Ho Chi Minh City, on which Jane (a friend from Neuchâtel) was the only woman among 30 men. She said that she had researched the weather and felt safe from typhoons and cyclones, but was presently "on a watch for pirates who rob freighters, no kidding. There is a narrow pass we are due to enter in early evening, which is where they often hang out. They are after cash of course, and also machinery etc."

Back at home finally, I wanted to take baths and showers constantly, I couldn't do it at Sara's for fear the kids would kill each other when I couldn't hear what was going on. Mark came in and found me in bed at 4 p.m. the first day I got back; wide awake, having a *major* senior moment, doing blissful nothing.

Chapter Eleven
Getting Old Ain't for Sissies

The building that had housed Spiral Pottery had to be re-possessed because Manuel defaulted on the mortgage. He had rented my building to a guy named Frank, who renovated the metal boxes that sold newspapers on street corners. Before they were painted, the

Al's messy car parts

boxes were sand blasted, and the sand filled the basement, the bathroom, and the drains. The sand was toxic because the paint had cadmium in it.

Manuel's building was rented to a very nasty middle European misogynist named Al, who was meaner than a pit bull. He didn't think wimmen should own buildings, and he hated artists in general. He liked cars, the noisier and smellier the better, in fact his whole business seemed centered upon revving engines to the max for as long as possible. Before Frank arrived on the scene, Al had filled the two back rooms of my building with oily old car parts. Mark went up to try and settle things, and Al threatened to kill him if he ever set foot on their property again.

Frank blocked the mutual driveway with a large compressor, Al phoned me daily to threaten that he was going to sue me for loss of business if I didn't move it. He wanted me to hire a tow truck, rip the air lines out of the compressor and move it somewhere else. When I called him, Frank yelled that he wasn't gonna move no goddam compressor and he was going after Al with a two by four. It was like the testosterone wars of the Middle East up there.

Finally I got rid of Frank, and went about the business of cleaning the building up so I could sell it. Sara's husband Andy was very helpful getting the contaminated sand removed. He hired people to unclog the drains, hired a truck to dispose of the sand, and knocked down a concrete block wall or two. The oily car parts also had to be removed. It cost me $40,000 to get the building presentable, and then I finally sold it for $116,000. It was such a relief to get rid of it that I didn't care about losing all that money!

During the week after Christmas 2000, Mark and I went with Mark's son Luke and his wife Ruth for a hair-raising visit with Mark's parents, Ella and Alan, in Maryland. The drive down took about eight hours, very snowy and fraught with accidents. Tractor trailers were turned upside down, Jeeps the wrong way round and jammed into guard rails, the flashing lights of ambulances, police, tow trucks, and great lines of cars waiting to go around the accidents made us all extremely nervous. It was such a relief to arrive safely that we hardly noticed the mess in the house that exceeded that of the famous Morley, King of Squalor.

We arrived around four-thirty in the afternoon, to find Ella wearing her pajamas, a dressing gown and a bib. She was anxious that Alan hadn't come back from walking the dog. Even the sudden descent of all the relatives couldn't get her away from the idea that something terrible had happened to him. He finally appeared with groceries. We had dinner on trays on our laps because the dining room table was groaning under a three year accumulation of papers, bills, Christmas cards, pills, corrugated boxes, staplers, tape, pens, cheque books, mortgage statements and health insurance forms. On the floor were two dried flower arrangements mixed in with dry dog food, elastic bands, staples, pens, animal hair. Well, you get the picture.

Ella was sliding into dementia, and Alan spent most of his time doing domestic chores, getting things for her, and looking after the dog and two cats. Patiently answering Ella's questions was time consuming too. The previous summer, he had said that he'd like to live in Jerusalem where he could practice his Hebrew, talking to Rabbis and immersing himself in the history of the Middle East. This visit, he said wistfully "If I have any time left, I think I'd like to live in Mexico."

They both slept in the living room in recliners because they couldn't get into the bedrooms. Apparently the living room had just been tidied up by other relatives in preparation for our visit, but there were still piles of stuff everywhere. At least we could sit down most of the time. Caleb, their Dalmatian, usually sat on the couch to keep an eye on the neighbour's dog. During our visit he was visibly annoyed by our sitting there.

197

Luke took a while to digest all of this bad information, but after a while he got his guitar out and sang to Grandma. Ruth was great; she found the rubber gloves and disinfectant and cleaned the bathroom.

I bought a filing system and attacked the piles of paper on the table, putting them in some sort of order so at least Alan could find things and keep track of bills. Under the table were about 20 cardboard boxes full of pills, from alfalfa to zinc, and everything in between. I lined them all up in alphabetical order on some shelves. When he came in, I said, "There, now you can see what you've got –you could open a shop!" And he said, "Oh great, now all our friends can see how many pills we take, they will think we are hypochondriacs! How embarrassing."

We broke down all the boxes and tied them up for recycling, got the table free enough of junk so I could wash it. Ella saw what I was doing and had a mini breakdown, trembling and crying, agitated by the change.

Downstairs in the basement, Mark tried to get the office in workable order so Alan could get to his computer and use his e-mail to keep in touch with people. There was a bad odour – I looked down at a paper bag full of dried cat turds, which he had every intention of throwing away. Housekeeping was definitely not easy for him. They were caught between the great depression when everything was saved, and the modern need to recycle everything. He must have had 75 dead batteries in 2 shoeboxes, but he didn't know what to do with them. With all our good intentions, I doubt that our youthful enthusiasm made any kind of a dent in their disturbing decline.

In May 2001, Mark and his older son Aaron went down to Maryland again because Alan had been hospitalized for meningitis. Mark was sleeping in his father's bed and when he got up he was covered in brown fuzzy things that he discovered were bits of foam from a disintegrating pillow. The sheet was in such bad shape that he threw it out, but there wasn't another one in the house!

At first the doctors thought Alan had had a stroke or concussion, then meningitis, but Aaron found a bill for an insecticide spraying company, researched it, and began to think that Alan had succumbed to the poison spray. The house was very dusty – cat hair, dog hair, tissue boxes full of dead nylon stockings, shoes that hadn't been moved for years, papers, books, letters, all pushed into corners so the piles of clothes on the bed could be reached. All the stuff caught the insecticide and held on to it. Alan and Ella were closed in the house with that poison all winter. The spray company came once a month, bugs or no bugs, and sprayed a synthetic pyrethrum with a half-life of six months. Ella's dementia could have been insecticide-induced nerve damage, too.

The doctors were not at all interested in hearing about Alan's insecticide exposure, as they had already decided it was bacterial meningitis in spite of not being able to get anything to grow in the lab from 3 successive spinal taps. They apparently were not taught in medical school that one of the known causes of meningitis is *chemical irritation of the meninges!* Mark slept two nights in Alan's bedroom and began to get monstrous pulsating headaches that were symptoms of meningitis.

Alan realized that he had to get out of the house, so finding a home with some meals available was the next step – thinking about cleaning out that house was scary! Maybe a few dumpsters on the front lawn would have done the trick. The house was mortgaged for considerably more than it was worth, in fact Alan wouldn't pay it off until he was 120 yrs old.

We hoped that they could get into a local retirement home, but Ella failed the capability test. It seemed like the perfect spot, because the fees were based on a percentage of their income, which meant that they could afford it. But she would have had to go into a separate facility, and he didn't like that. As a minister in the church, he married so many people that "Till Death Do Us Part" must have been ringing in his ears.

Ella finally went into a care facility, which was quite close to the house. She was bed ridden and not very interested in food, so she gradually died. With her, her pension and Alan's health insurance went to heaven, Alan was no longer able to cope with his payments, and he had to declare bankruptcy.

He went to stay with his daughter Kaaren and her husband Brian, who was a handsome devil, a military recruiter for the American war in Iraq. He disliked us with some intensity because Mark was a draft dodger back in the 60s and I am a Canadian. After a few months Kaaren and Brian brought Alan and Caleb, the Dalmatian, to us for a visit, but having driven for 8 hours to get here, wouldn't even stop to have dinner with us. They had to turn around and drive back, perhaps fearful that we might contaminate them. There was no discussion of when Alan would go back to live with them, and it gradually dawned on us that he had to make some decisions because he had no medical coverage in Canada. Caleb killed my vacuum cleaner with all those stiff little hairs. That dog and I were sworn enemies.

After a few months, Alan was invited to Bishop California by Ruth, a niece of Ella's, who lived in a trailer park there. Forty-five years ago, Alan had rescued her and her brother from an orphanage, where they were abandoned by their parents. They were children at the time, and Alan and Ella took care of them for a few years when they still lived in the States. Alan was nearly ninety when he moved to the mountains out west, and he enjoyed a few years dressing up for "Mule Days" celebrations, reading voraciously, and teaching Arabic to anyone who would listen.

A Three-Week High School Reunion

Mark and I rented our neighbour's house on the Spanish Costa Brava for three weeks in the fall of 2001 as a centre-point for a Neuchâtel reunion on a weekend at the end of September. Also invited to join us, were 3 women who were good friends 40 years ago. We planned a vacation that included a week in Spain, a drive to Switzerland for the reunion in Neuchâtel, and back to Spain for another week.

The Spanish house was built about 350 years ago – originally it had a stable on the main floor and living space above, the animals helped to keep the humans warm. In the last century, a renovation provided two bedrooms, kitchen, bathroom and sitting/dining rooms both upstairs and downstairs. It was like a whitewashed cave, with little windows in the back, and nice big windows in the front. There was a lovely tiled terrace on the roof, with a garden and a view of the Pyrenees in the distance. It only cost two hundred English pounds a week, so our shared expenses were not bad at all.

Heather came all the way from Australia. She never made her bed, hated health food, smoked and drank a lot, and she didn't look behind her. I thought she was morally superior because she took over all the thinking about food. She made rules every day; no talking about health or age related symptoms, no driving over the speed-limit, no driving with one hand, no wimping about food. She didn't mind conversations about makeup, tampons and my old boyfriends though.

Jane was a Quaker who had kept vigil over various hot spots in the world, spending time "witnessing" Native Indian strife in Canada and civilians in Iraq. She had volunteered for some very dangerous missions. We called her St. Jane the Intrepid. We all felt morally inferior to her, having never even considered such exploits.

Mark was the tour director, and he did most of the driving and navigating among the thousands of little cars tearing around like furious little bees. The roundabouts were like wild rides on the midway. He was a perfect saint. We wondered if people thought he had a harem, or if perhaps they thought he had been captured by Amazons. He threatened to sell us to every Mullah we saw if we didn't behave, and he often got big smiles and thumbs up from the Spanish men. Early in the trip, Jane wanted to lock all the car doors while we were on the highway. Heather and I objected to this because we thought it would be hard for anyone to rescue us from a flaming car if we had an accident. If she worried about abduction, we told Jane that we were sure they would take the women by the pound, so Heather would go first, then me. She was too skinny to be interesting to aliens.

I was the Border Collie, trying to keep track of everyone while they meandered through markets and shops buying stuff and getting lost trying to find bank machines. Trying to keep the flak down, I made a list of things to do while I waited for people. My best idea was to try and remember the lyrics of songs. That way, I could hum a little tune and not look completely bored or annoyed. They called me "Heil Mary" because I set leaving times, and gave out stern reminders.

In the first week, we drove down the coast to Tossa de Mar, a seaside village built around a medieval walled fortress. The drive down the coast was beautiful, a little ribbon of road winding back and forth above steep cliffs falling into the sea. No guardrails impeded our view. I was feeling quite seasick from the drive, so was infinitely glad to stop. We had a fabulous lunch in a restaurant hanging over the cliffs with a view of a little beach, fishing boats, some sunbathers leftover from the summer, and the sparkly Mediterranean. Our meal was a small mountain of fish, l'angostini, calamari, mussels, bread, wine and salad on great heaping plates. There was so much food that we had to use the next table to hold it all.

Our rental car was too small. Mark had to take his shoes off to drive because they were too big to fit between the pedals. We were driving to Neuchâtel to bring back our pal Susie, so we had to get a car that would fit all of us and our baggage. We had a map from Europcar, which gave the location of their office at a gas station in Gerona, so we headed there, through frantic traffic, all the streets going the wrong way, but we finally found Barcelona Street and eventually, the gas station. A sign in the window said that they had closed their office and relocated it at the train station. I was glad it didn't have a smiley face and "Have a Nice Day" at the bottom.

We navigated by Greek Chorus

"Oops left turn lane!"

"Go down there!"

"No! Over there!"

"There's the station! But how do we get there? It's one way!"

"Watch that car Mark, he's going to cut you off"

"Bloody stupid driver!"

Time was ticking away, of course, and we knew that everyone in Spain takes lunch from 1 to 5 in the afternoon with utter disregard for our needs.

Mark and I were left guarding the car because we couldn't find a legal parking spot. We waited and waited. Luckily, we were parked close to a wonderful lavabo, they have improved in Spain from a bottomless hole with a footpad and handles to a porcelain bowl which flushes. You can't get crabs because there are no toilet seats. Sometimes they are so modern that the flusher switch is disguised as a light switch, so if you press the wrong one you could bumble around in the dark for a long time.

Finally, after at least 45 minutes, I went to find Heather and Jane. I got to the Europcar office and they were gone. There was nobody in the office, it was closed for lunch. I thought they had been taken by the white slave trade, but Mark thought it was more likely to be alien abduction, but then he never went to Neuchatel Junior College where the girls had constant warnings about the perils of being jabbed with a hypodermic full of drugs and carried off, never to be seen again. So there we sat, out-worrying each other in the parking lot. It was mui humido.

Here's the story. A young woman wearing a huge car-accident neck-brace, sat behind the counter eagerly awaiting her lunch break. (*What* do the Spanish do for a four-hour lunch break?) She was in no mood to help these English speakers, and she said there were no cars available. Heather threatened to camp overnight in her office and sleep on her counter. It became obvious that Heather and Jane were not leaving.

And Jane said, "And what's more we came all the way from that office that you don't even have!"

And Heather said, "This is so bloody stupid! We specified from Canada that we needed five seats. This is your fault and you should fix it!"

Finally another officer arrived, fired up his computer and immediately found a suitable car right in his parking lot. It had to have the oil checked – that would take 5 hours, and we couldn't pick it up until six. Jane shook her finger at them and said, "We will return!"

Gerona is a beautiful ancient city, drenched in history. At every turn we were reminded of the presence of Romans, Visigoths, Arabs, and Jews living there in the middle ages. There's a lovely "Ramblas" lined with huge old Plane trees where we had a great lunch and enjoyed an hour of people watching. We visited the Jewish quarter with streets too narrow for cars, the Jewish Museum and the Arab Baths, where we picked up an interesting new vocabulary –tepidarium, frigidarium and calderium.

We got back to Europcar around 6 and it took another hour. They had to re-do everything. Although we all believed that Heather and Jane had driving privileges from the previous week, this was incorrect. They had to present passports and driving licenses, information had to be typed in, and checked over and over. Finally we had a car with five seats; we were belted in, prepared to launch ourselves into the traffic frenzy. Mark could wear his sandals while driving, but he wanted the car to reverse, and he couldn't get the gearshift to work.

"Push it in!"

"Pull it out!"

"Pull it up!"

"Try double clutching!"

"Bloody stupid CAR!"

Mark was wrestling the gearshift with two hands as Heather jumped out and went to find the agent. It was so simple, lift the knob up, it slips right into reverse. The agent had a good laugh as he said, "What do you expect from a French car?" When we stopped to fill up with gas we couldn't get the flap over the gas cap to open. We took apart the front seat looking for a lifter knob that would open it. We each examined the dashboard. Finally the gas station attendant came over, shut all the car doors, used the remote entry system to lock and then unlock the doors, and the gas flap!

It took three days to drive to Neuchâtel because we wanted to see the countryside and dawdle a bit, so we had time for some fantastic meals, seafood in Provence, morelle soup and rosti potatoes, local patés and wine. Heather was appalled at the number of times Mark ordered pizza, and after she finished berating him, he said that he was on a private "Pizza Tour" of Europe and to leave him alone.

We arrived in Neuchâtel on Friday afternoon, just in time for a typically Swiss dinner. We couldn't figure out what it was. Forty years ago we used to say that dinner was veal disguised as shoe leather. This was pink like fish, but it had the wrong texture – it was served with boiled cabbage – I'll say no more. It didn't matter because the Fete de Vindages started that night with bands playing, confetti everywhere, rides, dancing in the streets, hawkers, wine and beer flowing on every corner until after two in the morning. We drank too much wine and laughed ourselves silly. We heard a story about our late comrade Hoagy, whose girlfriend's mother complained about the shot spots on her couch in the basement. Hoagy solemnly blamed the dog, so the mother had the dog put down. Hoagy had to stop seeing the girl after that because he felt so guilty.

Red told us that at Christmas he failed every subject, and he was given a detention every Saturday morning with Monsieur Bubloz, the French teacher. After two weeks, Red commiserated with Monsieur Bubloz, saying that it was unfair for them both to stay home from skiing. Monsieur Bubloz was being punished too! They made a compromise, and they went skiing every Saturday as long as Red spoke French the whole time, and of course they had to go places where they wouldn't see Mr. Wilde, or any of us.

After two days of partying, people started to drift off to other adventures, and we left Monday morning in a big hurry to get to Carcasonne by Tuesday afternoon. We took Susie with us, whose first rule was, "No PDA!" which meant "no public displays of affection". It was a shot across the bow of the only married couple. We zoomed down the Rhone River Valley with Stirling Moss at the wheel. As we approached three huge concrete towers, Mark commented on their beautiful shapes - hyperbolic paraboloids. Oh my God, said Jane, it's one of those awful nuclear plants! It is killing everything in the river!

"Oh no, said Susie, it's a lovely big ceramics factory, those are the furnaces! I've seen them in England!" Of course it was a huge nuclear plant, and it had a stone marker to tell us how benign and healthful it was.

That night we stayed in Nimes, which had a marvelous Roman amphitheater, a wonderful market full of mushrooms and fish, and beautiful shops with linens and wools from Provence. We hated to leave in the morning before the shops opened, but as we zoomed out of town on the highway, it was fascinating to hear Heather contact her bank in Australia on her cell phone. She had to straighten out some VISA problem, she talked to several different people and solved the situation while speeding along in the back seat of the car.

Carcasonne has been inhabited since 600 BC, and it is a very impressive walled city with a moat, huge turrets and cobbled streets. We could see it perched high up on a hill from miles away. Heather found a restaurant in her guidebook, which served a fabulous cassoulet for lunch. In the parking lot there were about twenty caravans parked every which-way. Laundry was hanging everywhere, and bedding aired in the sun. Old women cooked lunch over open fires; young women with henna hair swarmed Mark and tried to inveigle him to join them for their siesta. Luckily his tribe of Amazons saved him from the gypsies. They even dyed their poodle with henna.

Jane, Mary, Susie, Heather

Back in Spain we tried to go to the Terra Cotta Museum in La Bispal, but it was never open, in spite of what the sign said. Instead we meandered through the clay market, amazed at the number of clay shops and the variety of work, some of it from Portugal. La Bispal was also close to Ullastret, a fortified city with beautiful views overlooking the fertile plain, fields of corn, sugar cane, a castle in the distance. Ullastret had a museum full of Roman and Greek pottery as well as a contemporary ceramic artist who opened her shop for us for five hurried minutes. After October first, restaurants and tourist attractions shut their doors firmly. They don't bother to warn you beforehand. You can't blame them, the hoards of English and German tourists unloading from buses were quite intimidating even in September. A couple of times we were the only people in a restaurant, but they still could produce a feast of fresh eel, hake, l'angostini, all kinds of paella, paté, and wonderful cheeses. In Regencos we drank local wine that cost $1.75 a litre.

As a group, we became more adept at avoiding contentious issues, and slowly the electric party atmosphere wore down. We spent the last day cleaning up the house, packing, and in the evening we went to a café on the beach for a glass of wine and a last envious look at the locals. We ate as many leftovers as we could, and drank an amazing assortment of leftover alcohol; walnut liqueur, peach snaps, whiskey, gin, wine…we had a lot of toasts to make.

Mark and I were glad to get back to Ontario, geronting along in our quiet little space in the country, feeling extremely well adjusted, smart, and really quite smug!

Beth and David with the twins and Brooke

We had a very funny Christmas, entertainment provided by my offspring.

Beth and David arrived for lunch on Christmas Eve with the adorable twins, Charlie and T.J., who were two-and-a-half years old. They were learning to call me "Granny-Green-Car" to distinguish me from David's mother, also called Granny. The boys wanted to discover every childproof thing that I had forgotten. They made up a game of running walnuts in their shells through a tube left over from Christmas wrapping paper. The nuts acted like giant ball bearings and lurked in odd places for months. Miraculously we didn't step on one in the middle of the night after the cat's midnight hockey game. My rowing machine had a seat that slid back and forth, catching tiny fingers. I gave them rides, one at a time, but the other one was disconsolate and screamed. At one point, they both ended up in the (dry) bathtub eating soap. David picked up letters and Christmas cards and read them out like a stentorian camp announcement, he interviewed people, he threw the twins in the air making them scream, then he made a huge amount of noise on Mark's bongo drums. Just afterward, he said,

"It's really quiet here, I love it" as he fell asleep on the couch.

On Christmas Day, we drove across country to the east and north to Sara and Andy's cottage at Minden. When we got to the cottage, skidoo tracks were evident in the snow, footprints walking up to the window and around the house, and an alarm sounding anxiously from within. Signs of a boogey man, I thought, but it turned out to be friends who had started a fire in the fireplace to warm the place up, and the fire alarm was just getting exercise.

I was in charge of getting the turkey stuffed and in the oven, then the Christmas pie. A tradition of Mum's, involving place cards, strings, entertaining presents at the end of the strings, and a centerpiece in the middle of the table, which conceals the presents. For Sara there was "The Bad Girls Book". She nearly choked, she laughed so hard. One of the plans was to have a winter tan party – get posters from the travel agent, wear bikinis, have beach boys slather on the tanning lotion for ultra violet lamps. Whole coconuts, machetes and live crabs would decorate the apartment, with sand on the floor, and the furnace turned up. Wicked tropical drinks with little umbrellas would be served, and aqua dye put in the bathtub water for skinny-dipping.

Mark made a ceramic chicken cooker for Andy, a tapered cylinder about 8 inches high which the cook fills with beer, wine, juice, or all three; garlic, herbs, etc. The raw whole chicken is impaled upon it for cooking on the grill, and the meat is suffused with flavour and moistness. It's better than a beer can because of the aluminum and paint on the can and the plastic liner. Trying to come up with a polite name was difficult! Andy wanted to call it *"The Chicāno* - put a volcano of flavour in your chicken" (Has to be pronounced with a hard *ā*, not to be confused with Mexicanos in America). Also *"The Chicken Stance"*, *"Chick Dick"*, *"Chicken Seteee"*, *"Chicken Diddle by Chicken Little"* (Mark's nickname), *"Chicken up the Wazoo"* and *"Chicken Styletes"* after St. Simon the pole sitter.

Mikey, still the most gorgeous person on the planet, even with missing laterals and eyeteeth, demanded a bath with his buddy, Hudson, at about 6 P.M. They closed the bathroom door and had about an hour doing hydraulics lab. Then Mikey opened the door and yelled "Granny!!!! I need my ROBE!!!" So we put it on with nothing underneath, and he came to the Christmas dinner table thusly attired, with his wet hair slicked back.

"Well Hello there, Heff" said his father.

"Don't call me Heff!" said Mikey.

"O.K. *Hugh*", said his father.

The dinner proceeded apace, and I barely avoided setting the place on fire. Mum always poured warm brandy over the English fruit pudding to set it alight – but I put a bit too much on, and then tipped the plate bit too much so the flaming Brandy almost flowed off onto the table. (Gravity was always a point of contention at that house; Mikey had often been heard stomping around yelling, "I hate gravity!") I was extremely lucky not to have set the house on fire by pouring flaming brandy on to the beautiful red jacquard tablecloth.

On Boxing Day I was having a shower at about 10AM, and could hear Sara crabbing away at Andy. He had cleaned up after Christmas dinner, done all the dishes, saved all the meat from the bones, but thrown the carcass out. A cardinal sin! In Sara's mind, she was going to feed everyone turkey soup for the next millennium.

"She's being mean to me Mary!"

"Well Andy, it's before noon – after fifteen years, why haven't you figured out that Sara hates the morning?"

To Sara I said,

"Just be a bad girl and get the carcass out of the garbage, there's a lot of great leftovers in there. But then there were cigarette butts and coffee grounds, and too many witnesses. It reminded me of my sister Annie feeding cat food on Triscuits to various people in the family – maybe *she* actually wrote the book for bad girls.

The Gardiner Museum had invited me to submit to an invitational show called "The Mad Hatter's Tea Party" to add Canadian contemporary work to a show called "The Artful Teapot". I made The Mad Hatter and The March Hare as teapots. These teapots were about a foot high, and were modeled after the original illustrations in Alice and Wonderland. The heads are the teapot lids, one arm a handle, the other the spout. The Mad Hatter is wearing spats, which I had to research, buttons on the outside, elastic

212

underneath? How high up the ankle? And what was their purpose? I never thought I'd be doing spat research.

March Hare and Mad Hatter Teapots

Both teapots were bought by Sonny and Gloria Kamm from whose vast collection Garth Clark had developed the show "The Artful Teapot". The Kamms have a whole apartment reserved for their collection of teapots.

Chapter Twelve
Feeling Like The Evil Fairy

I don't think my family was prejudiced against black people, Chinese, or Jews, but for some reason they hated Catholics. Aunt Beth, who was considered to be an intellectual giantess, once told me that she spent a considerable amount of time in the grocery store turning the soup cans so the English side would show instead of the French. She was convinced that there was a conspiracy of Catholics to show the French side. Then she would point out that our last 5 Canadian Prime Ministers were Catholic, as though that fact tied in with the soup can conspiracy.

When Sara married into an Italian Catholic family, she told the priest that she had been baptized in the Boyne River, by her god-parents and her parents. The priest asked if we had said the right words. Sara was about six months old when we dipped her in the Boyne, but she assured the priest that we had said the right words, so she was allowed to marry in the Catholic Church. Now I know we should have put salt on her tongue to keep the devil out, but never mind. She did promise to bring her children up as Catholics.

When my girls were very young, their paternal Grandfather wanted me to have them baptized, but I thought they should choose their own religion, not to be forced into something that might not agree with them. I asked him if he thought my girls were conceived in sin. No he didn't. Then I asked if he thought they would go to Limbo if they were killed in a car crash. He didn't think they would go to Limbo, but he did say that in life one has to take care of the things that one has, he had insurance on his car, his house and his life, for instance. I was appalled and accused him of being a terrible hypocrite for wanting God Insurance on my children.

In 1998, Sara and her family moved to Bolton Ontario, a hot bed of Italian Catholic activity, and all of her children went to the local Catholic School. Their father, Andy, a busy film director working in Halifax, didn't take much interest in their Catholic upbringing. When something scared him or made him feel guilty, he got absolution from a priest or two, but otherwise he was not bothered to go to church.

The baptism part wasn't too onerous. Sara didn't want to take too much time off the sunny dock to get a dress for Mia, so she bought a dress from Stedman's, a local five and dime store. The dress was flimsy and bit trashy, but Mia loved it.

Mia's older brother Mathew disliked his religion class, and he would have been required to have his first Communion in grade eight, because they do kids his age every other year. Mathew gave us a harangue on how much time they wasted learning about the Bible and concluded with, "My friends get $5000.00 when they have their first Communion, so that's what I'll get too." I told him that if he's in it for the money, he should change to Judaism because boys get tons more than that when they are thirteen at their Bar Mitzvah.

Mamma Mia and what do I know?? Along comes First Communion. I remember visiting the huge piazza in front of the

Gothic Cathedral in Milan May of 1960 - it was absolutely full of 8-year-old girls in tiny wedding dresses. It's a sight I'll never forget. Probably for that reason, I decided to make Mia's dress, so that she wouldn't look too much like a bride. It had to be white. I thought maybe at eight years old, they feared that she would never have another chance to dress up like a virgin. Her Catholic grandmother said that Mia needed more fear in her life, and for that reason Catholicism was a good thing. She instructed me to make the dress because I could sew. Communion dresses were very expensive to buy, and she didn't want the aggravation of shopping for one. She told me to dress Mia like a bride, with a veil. My mother wouldn't let me have a white dress, a veil, or a wedding cake when I married Mia's grandad, because I was a bit pregnant, so I knew about that symbolism.

Time passed. We thought she was getting instruction at school, we thought she was learning about her sins. The Laziers have been protesting Protestants for five hundred years, but we busied ourselves making the dress and getting the shoes. Some of us discussed lovely gifts we could give her for First Communion –a nice big light up crucifix for the front hall, a shrine for the front lawn, or a Velasquez painting of the crucifixion.

On Mother's Day, Sara went to a spa with a friend, and when Andy came home from Halifax for the weekend, he had to take Mia to the church for "Reconciliation". Andy had arrived with jet lag on Friday night, drove for 3 hours to the cottage with three kids, drove back in time to get Mia to the church, and all for naught. The priest was from India, where they have more control over the children. I am sure they are more devout too. He said Mia could not make her first confession because she did not know right words. Andy did a hilarious imitation of his East Indian accent " It's veddy, veddy bad, she does not know the correct words, she cannot make good confession." He sounded just like Deepak Chopra

Poor Mia was rejected by God. Poor me, I had made that nice dress all the while being appalled by eating the flesh and drinking the blood in a virginal white dress - poor Andy felt like a terrible father not to have been there to instruct her. That evening, Mia produced her religion textbook, a full colour booklet, comic book style, with stories of Matthew, Simon, and all the Apostles, and I spent the evening of Mother's Day reading the stories to Sara. I told Andy that I was finally giving my daughter some religious instruction.

On Monday, Sara went to the school and had a teensy weensy fit. The school priest, Father Bob, apologized profusely to Mia, and to Sara. He promised that they would teach her the right words before Thursday when the First Communion would be celebrated. Mia had her first confession on Wednesday, and her penance was to hug her mother. She actually had three penances but we don't know what the other two were.

Then it was Thursday, and Sara told me that I would have to sit in church with Andy's parents who hate me because I've been divorced (and they don't even know how many times). What would the bad heathen granny wear not to be mistaken for the Evil Fairy? I don't own a church-going hat. I expected that in church, they would be splashing holy water, rattling rosaries, popping up and down on their knees, breathing the incense and listening to sermons about how guilty we all are. Unless Mathew declared a conflict of interest and I could stay home to baby-sit him, I knew I was in for it.

Mathew tried every trick he knew to persuade his parents that he couldn't go, and I offered to stay home with him, but Andy in a suit looks like a Mafia don. We do what he says. We went. Mia had her hair done up on top of her head with sparkles and ringlets, her dress looked great. People were very casual about their dress in church, we

218

even saw a person in a tracksuit. No incense, no holy water, no rosaries, and nobody looked askance at me. Father Bob actually loves children and he was wearing Hush Puppies and a plaid flannelette shirt under his white Surplice.

Ireland

I went to Ireland with Nancy Roach, my roommate at Boston University forty years ago. She had visited the Emerald Isle eight times previously, so it seemed natural that she would plan our visit.

Driving in Ireland on the wrong side of the road is an experience in itself. Nancy had had a knee replacement before our trip, so it was vital for us to have an automatic car. It was a great relief not to have to think about shifting gears while zooming around a fearsome round-about in the fog, dodging the huge lorries and cars like swarming ants, attempting to decide which lane to be in, and how and where to get off. Our itinerary included several castles, a few palaces, and many great houses full of tapestries, baronial antique mahogany furniture, ornate plaster ceilings, portraits, and for me, fabulous long bathtubs of generous width and sloping backs. I especially loved the decadence of combining Irish whiskey with the bathtub at the end of a long day.

Adare was a good place to stay the first night after arriving by plane at Shannon. It was an adorable town with thatched cottages and lots of cows and sheep in a churchyard. It was interesting to see the ancient stone cottages still in use. There were a few new houses with interesting thatches around upper windows, quite like very thick bangs. In fact it was similar to the town Tullymore, in the film "Waking Ned Divine" but that skinny little Michael O'Sullivan was not careening through the town, stark bare-naked on his motor cycle.

Connemara was the real beginning of our trip, featuring huge Rhododendron trees, Azaleas in yellows and oranges, fruit trees in bloom, tulips running wild all over. Daisies, Fritillaria, and Delphiniums were all robust and truly lovely. The gardens were at least a month ahead of Canada. On the way north we visited "Coole" the estate of Lady Augusta Gregory who must have died fifty years ago, but a letter came for her in the mail that very day. Her garden was in spring beauty, with a fabulous Copper Beech carrying the initials of many famous Irish writers and poets. W B. Yeats was among her admirers, and he spent a lot of time there in a castle tower. I was reading Brenda Maddox's biography of Yeats, George's Ghosts a fascinating account of how his wife George controlled him by automatic writing. A husband would have to believe in the spirits for this to work, but she told him all kinds of intimate things through automatic writing, how to behave properly, who their friends should be, how and when to make love to her. W.B.Y. defined gullibility.

We stayed at a lovely country house in Cashel, built around 1850, which had horses arriving at 2 AM, with loud clopping on the cobbled courtyard outside the window, and horses whinnying greetings to each other. The estate had quite a collection of geese, ducks, sheep, horses, and an enormous kitchen garden. Divine smelling peat fires burned in the great rooms, which were comfortably furnished with chintz armchairs and portraits of horses and horsey Englishmen with pinheads (never sure if they had pin heads in reality or if the painters took more interest in costumes, medals, jewelry and other accoutrements). We drove around the western edge of Connemara, populated by rocks, fishing boats, very small colourful stucco houses, and a lot more rocks. We visited Kylemore Abbey. It seemed forbidding; more so when one realized that it was a secluded Catholic school for girls who were well behaved 24 hours a day. No visitors allowed.

Here is a typical Irish weather forecast.

"Today will be a coolish, windy day with sunshine and showers, with the risk of some heavy thundery ones. The showers may merge to give a longer spell of rain in the far north for a time in the morning. Strong and gusty west to southwest winds will tend to moderate later in the day and back southwesterly. Later in the day cloud will increase in the south-west bringing outbreaks of rain". Sometimes they said things like "Freshening southeast winds will steadily bring clouds northeast across most parts.

The Irish are swept away by soccer, and the big news was that their best player had gotten into an altercation with the team manager and in a fit of rage hurled the insult that his father was an Englishman. He was sent home in disgrace. The day after, he had an hour interview to make himself look innocent, pleading that it was unfair that the spat was published, that he wanted to play for Ireland but it seemed unlikely that he would in fact apologize. All the waiters in the bar were hiding behind the potted palms so they could see the TV without being seen.

Galway was next, and we were looking for a musical evening because there hadn't been any entertainment out in the country. The pubs didn't start the music until 9:30 or so and by that time we were horizontal. In Galway we stayed at a hotel right down town on a cobbled street with traffic excluded. It was lovely to walk freely on these ancient streets admiring bookstores, pubs, and wool shops. Galway Bay was full of swans, the shops were painted bright colours, the people seemed pleased with themselves. May was a great time to be traveling, not just because it was beautiful in the spring, but also not too crowded with tourists. We couldn't find any pub music, so it was a treat to be serenaded for about an hour by a young man who played the saxophone under our hotel window. The cobbled streets and stone storefronts made a lovely acoustical reverberation. He had a charming repertoire which included "Summertime", "Ain't Misbehavin" and "Keeps Rainin' all the Time" (which it did).

The Burren, on the west coast, was a barren expanse of limestone rock with small rocks, big rocks, rock walls, rock cairns, and rock houses. It looked like an enormous concrete mountain from a distance, but driving close to it, the details were amazing. The cracks in the rock are called "grykes" and in them, arctic and alpine flowers grew along with 50 species of orchids. The grykes ranged in depth from one foot to twenty feet in depth; they separated the "clints", which were big smooth flat rectangular sheets of limestone. Soil in the grykes was created by dead plant material, weathered limestone, and wind-born silt. The rocks held a lot of heat, which encouraged small plants, and the grykes held water as well.

By this time I was well immersed in Gaelic pronunciation, driving on the wrong side of the road, Irish history and the here-to-fore unsuspected evilness of the English. Pronunciation was a big issue because Nancy had studied Irish Gaelic in University and she confessed that being Irish was her main hobby. Nancy was learning from me that I don't share tastes of my dinner. It seems unsanitary, (double dipping) messy, and rude to have a person reach across the table to remove hunks of my dinner. If Mark did that I'd stab him with my fork!

The great piles of crenellations, mahogany, portraits and plaster ceilings were leftovers from the Protestant Irish who had been loyal to the English King. Glin Castle was owned by the Knight of Glin. As we were arriving, a big ruddy Englishman tried to herd me onto his bus, "Into the bus girlie!" he cried as he pawed my front. Another red faced old fart tried to stop Nancy from signing the register. "Too dangerous to sign things!" he said. We were thrilled that they were leaving, because in the crush of bodies in the foyer, they seemed to have been arriving. The estate is about 500 acres, right on the Shannon River, a huge walled garden full of vegetables and pansies for the salads. After dinner we had a nightcap by the peat fire and some Americans remarked that we must be very brave to be driving a car on those narrow roads. But we thought it wasn't the driver who was brave, it was the passenger. Luckily, our left mirror was hinged; it acted like cat's whiskers for us, flipping in whenever we got too close on the left side. We had to straighten it out about 4 times a day. This same lady warned us not to take the route Nancy was planning through the "Connor Pass". Luckily no big tour buses or trucks use this route because it is extremely narrow and curvaceous, with very few guard rails and many precipitous views with no road visible below. Being on the outside was harrowing.

The Dingle was worth it though, a delightful seaside town with a pet dolphin who swam in and out with the fishing boats. The town was touristy, but also a great fishing village with a nice pub for evening music. Driving around the peninsula, we came upon some interesting "beehive huts" built by "corbelling", a method of building which layers flat stones with a downward and outward tilt to shed rain,

A "beehive" hut

and at the top, the shape was closed with one flat rock. The huts have been standing for centuries, some people think that monks used them for shelter, others think they were used by farmers from ancient times to about 1200AD. Whoever used them had a spectacular view over the sea to the west if the fog ever lifted.

Lunch that day was in a local pub where we hardly stuck out at all, two well dressed Americanae Corpulentae in a Breugel painting of rheumy ancient toothless men and women drinking Guinness in the darkness. After a while a small child came in and ordered two old crones to go out to a waiting car. The old ladies had a vociferous finger-pointing fight on the way out, much to the amusement of the waitress, who said they were sisters and fought all the time. That's why they never sat together. In fact most of the customers sat alone staring into space, but the village was so small they all must have known each other.

That night we stayed at a Best Western, for which Nancy apologized a number of times (NQOCD = not quite our class dear), but we had a fantastic evening of music with some American travelers who could dance to everything. They must have been trained in Irish dancing as kids; the men were especially fast and light-footed.

The drive to Bantry would have been spectacularly beautiful if we could have seen it through the rain and incredibly dense fog.

"It will be very changeable throughout the coming week. Another band of rain will move across the country from the west on Monday, some of the rain will be heavy and persistent. It will also be breezy. There may be a little sunshine on Tuesday before further cloudy and damp conditions affect most parts once again. The wind will also pick up,

Bantry House

especially along coasts. There will be showery conditions Wednesday and Thursday, but also the chance of a few brighter spells. Friday will be at risk for more cloud and showers."

In spite of the weather, Bantry House was absolutely fabulous. Owned by the Earls of Bantry since 1739, it is a museum of 19th century furniture, paintings, and a marvelous formal Italian garden with a noisy fountain. Wisteria curled around the window, the fountain splashed away, the bathtub was not just long wide and deep, but it had a spot for the Whiskey glass, it got two prizes at once from me. An amazing sleep. The house faces Bantry Bay, full of blue water, sail boats and a rather suspicious oil derrick. We often saw road signs that indicated that the ECC had contributed to the finances of construction. Seeing the oil derrick, I wondered if this was how the Irish paid. I had kippers for breakfast. The Marmalade was excellent: bitter, not too much jelly, roughly chopped, not too sweet, it definitely won all prizes.

Lots more sheep on the drive down to the south coast. There seem to be no natural forests or predators, so the sheep proliferate like there's no tomorrow. We saw the Dromberg Circle, 17 huge stones set 4 to 5000 years ago to record the winter solstice. The stones are big and solemn, standing in a farmer's field; they speak of the ancient Celtic people and their astonishing knowledge and strength. Perhaps there is an ancient civilization buried there, but it seems that the stones stand alone, facing the sea, bearing the elements forever.

On to Cashel, this one in County Tipperary, another grand house, and a wet walk to the Rock of Cashel, an amazing dinner of scallops, and salad presented between two lacy discs of fried Parmesan cheese. The six scallops were in a circle around the salad, interspersed with dollops of mayonnaise blended with pesto. We had so many fabulous dinners on this trip that I thought I would need to hire a forklift to get me onto the plane home.

In Kilkenny we were amazed at the activities and the wealth of the craft council. In Ireland, the crafts people are recognized as part of the economy, a major reason why visitors go there. Canada should take a hint here. There was a huge castle and part of it was an ancient stable which had been turned into 2 very impressive craft shops, with studios behind, so that one could visit people at work making pottery, jewelry, weaving, knitting and "all sorts of everything" as the concierge at the hotel commented. The castle had been owned by the Butler family, whose ancestor was apparently the butler to an English King. As well as being the butler, he was the wine steward and got 10% of each shipment.

At Newgrange the weather deteriorated so much that our guide to the site screamed into the gale

"Are we all mad? Glory be to God, I'll be the first Irishwoman in space!"

Newgrange was built a thousand years before the pyramids of Giza. The mound is 90 meters in diameter, and with its standing stones, covers an area of almost an acre. The roof is constructed by corbelling: huge slabs of rock, each one partly rests on the one below. Six meters from the floor a single slab seals the roof. It is speculated that the cremated remains of people were put in the tomb until the winter solstice, when the sun shone into the passage leading into the center for 4 days. With careful measurements, they would have been able to see that the sun appeared to be reversing its direction, and they believed that the souls of the cremated would be taken by the returning sun. Our guide gave us a stunning re-enactment of the path of light shining into the main passage as it does at the winter solstice. It would indeed be a "Glory be to God week" if the sun actually shone for 4 consecutive days. The inside of the structure was decorated with concentric circles, diamonds and chevrons carved into the rock.

Four days in Dublin, two glorious bus rides on the top of a double-decker, visits to great shopping on Grafton Street, a tour of the sites of the Easter rebellion of 1916, and afterwards a Guinness with the tour leader.

On our last night in Ireland we saw the most amazing thing I have ever seen on TV. The Eurovision Song Contest, in which singers from all over Europe compete for awards, given by a phone-in audience. We saw three Slovenian transvestites, previously known as the "Suspender Sisters". Dressed as air hostesses, they wore pink sequined suits with very short skirts, pantyhose, and size 12 pumps,

227

with little airline hats to match. Their back-up singers were short males, dressed as pilots, in beige, with pilot caps as well. The intermission entertainment was a dance troupe of half naked men beating themselves with branches.

A stunning end to a fabulous trip. We laughed ourselves to sleep.

Chapter 13
On My Mary Way

We suffered from "Travelitis Nervosa" before our trip to Costa Rica. I read William Deverell's <u>The Laughing Falcon</u> about a nice Canadian woman who went to Costa Rica for a holiday and got kidnapped by a revolutionary band called the "Cinco de Mayo". Costa Rica is right there between the Contras and the Sandinistas.

Of course our friends and family had admonitions about the tropics too.

> *Spiders, snakes and poisonous frogs,*
>
> *Mosquitoes, Malaria, bats and bogs,*
>
> *Erupting volcanoes with rivers of ash,*
>
> *Will we ever get home, I thought in a flash.*

It was a Canadian Wildlife Tour, run by Quest International, and they sent us a long list of unguents, itch powders, pain-killers, damp towelettes, blister pads, mosquito repellent, Immodium, Pepto Bismol, et cetera. Packing the drug store took a whole extra bag, and made me yet more apprehensive.

The first day was spent in transit. In NYC the airlines threatened us. Since they had overbooked, they were pleading with people to stay in a hotel overnight. Then they told us that the incoming plane was late, and if we didn't hurry up and get in our seats nicely, then our plane would have to land in Panama City because San Jose Airport closed for construction at 10PM. It turned out well, we stayed in a very civilized hotel surrounded by bougainvillea, and a gorgeous tropical garden. The local roosters woke everyone up at 3 AM.

The next day we flew around the mountains to the south of San Jose, and down the coast to the southernmost tip of Costa Rica. Our planes were tiny 6-seaters, and the trip took just over an hour. From the air, Tiskanita Jungle Lodge and the airstrip were invisible, but the ocean and beach were clear, beautiful and completely devoid of human habitation. The landing strip was just a bit of mowed grass.

The lodge was up a big hill, our first major climb, but it was softened by the sight of wild hibiscus, impatiens, several large iguanas sunning themselves, and brilliant birds flitting through the jungle. It was hot and sunny, about 90 degrees and very humid. That afternoon we went for our first jungle walk to get us acclimatized. Our guide was Leopold Chavez, a native born Costa Rican, who carried binoculars and a monocular scope everywhere he went. He had remarkable eyes and ears; he could see birds and monkeys a hundred yards away.

The owner of the Jungle Lodge was reforesting his property with mahogany and various palms, plus a wonderful orchard growing ugli fruit and star fruit. He owned about 600 acres, and most of it was original jungle. The trees grew incredibly fast, and the Costa Ricans made fences by cutting lengths of trees, about a fence post long, then stuck them in the ground, stapled on some barbed wire, and a new tree grew out of the stump.

Our room at Tiskanita had screens; the bathroom had no screens or outside wall. I thought we might be visited by snakes or wild monkeys, but only a small iguana came to admire himself in the mirror. Up in the woods there were macaws in a cage, a couple of American girls were looking after them, hoping to release them into the wild. Early every morning Leo set up his scope near the pool, to look at the birds.

On the morning of day four we flew back to San Jose and the bus took us to Le Paz, where there is a stunning butterfly garden. We walked down several flights of metal stairs to see four major waterfalls. Engineering feats of the jungle are truly amazing, just locating where the stairs would go in the jungle would be difficult, but building them to fit the steep slopes and supporting them must have taken the talents of a great team. We saw morpho butterflies there, bright blue with a wingspan of about 6 inches. We also saw owl eye and Phoebis butterflies.

The road to the Arenal Volcano was typical of the next few days. To build a road, a big machine carves out the side of the mountain. A truck pours on a pile of rocks, the size of which varies from sand to a small chicken. The rocks are rolled into the matrix of dirt and there you have a road. Unfortunately, there is a great deal of rain which washes away all the fine particles and the road is left with pot holes that a horse could snooze in, and bumps the size of giant turtles. A trip in a vehicle is like riding a bucking bronco. Sitting up straight, you can gallop along. But don't lean back! You'll fall on the floor.

The morning we arrived, the volcano was shrouded in cloud. Leo used a branch of a tree to make a bird feeding station; he put fresh fruit on all the twigs, and hauled it up by rope to hang about 4 feet down from a live tree branch, 20 feet from the ground. Some very nice looking animals began to congregate. They were coatis, long and slim with beautiful long tails, a face like a skunk, they reminded me of raccoons. There were about 15 of them, and I asked Leo if they ever figured out his feeding station, thinking of how clever Canadian squirrels are. He said he had never seen that happen. Soon the coati leader was up the tree, pacing along the main branch over the feeder. He was doing the math. Then he shimmied down the rope, grabbed some fruit and shimmied back up again. The others learned fast and followed suit. The birds at the feeder were marvelous; all kinds of tanagers, hepatic, palm, grey, blue, as well as red legged honeycreepers and clay coloured robins.

As the morning wore on, the mist cleared, we could see smoke billowing out of the top of Mount Arenal, and we heard a few growls from the volcano. In the evening we went much closer in the bus, to see the lava flow. On the way, Leo said,

"We will just stop here to see if we can see the white parrot". Sure enough, he set up his scope and about 75 yards away there was a tree with a hole in it, and in the hole, there sat a white parrot. I was pretty sure it was stuffed for the tourists, but then it moved. Maybe he moved it by remote control.

The volcano sent out red-hot rocks at intervals, great shouts went up from the 75 or so people sitting on our lookout point. It was like watching fireworks.

From Arenal we bumped over to Monteverde in the bus. We had the most extraordinary room at our hotel, "Fonda Vela". It was over 30 feet long, with a bay window, and a bath that was 6 feet long. The ceiling and the floor were both made of mahogany, and the mahogany furniture was built to fit the room. There was a comfortable reading couch, a chair, coffee table, desk, vanity, wardrobe, chest of drawers, and two double beds. We had found a T-shirt, which said, "I survived the road to Monteverde". With the terrible roads, one expected the worst accommodations!

We arrived in Monteverde by 5 PM for a lecture by a local guide. He told us that there were two kinds of birds: SYBs (small yellow birds) and LBJs (little brown jobs). Because it is the cloud forest, the jungle is very wet and drippy. The huge trees were absolutely covered with moss and epiphytes of all sorts including orchids and bromeliads. At one point, we were standing on a suspension bridge with our group of 20 (WARNING: no more than 20 people allowed on this bridge!) when another large group of people arrived. Their guide started to howl like an alpha male monkey, addressing the monkeys we were watching, and their alpha male leader started up quite a fierce argument with him. Apparently a band of monkeys can be attacked by a roving alpha male, and if the wild one kills the leader of the pack, he will also kill all the babies, so he can start his own genetic line.

The bravest thing I ever did in my life was to go on the "SkyTrek" cable ride, which took us 500 feet in the air, speeding along at about 25 miles an hour for a distance of 700 feet, in one case. The ad says:

"It is natural that people seek and marvel at the unknown. An adventure with mysterious and unfamiliar places and life forms inspires emotion, sometimes fear. Those people who overcome their fears and those who push their limits are richly rewarded with new and satisfying discoveries of the natural world."

It didn't say anything about climbing 1200 feet vertically in a 4 Km hike: nothing about climbing two towers of 100 feet, or the 60 mph wind that blows up there. We were outfitted with harnesses, which had huge clips to attach to the giant zip line. We also had gloves and a hard hat. From a platform, we were attached to the cable and pushed off into a cloud. There was a handsome young man at the end of the ride to catch each person, so they wouldn't run into a large cement pole that suspended the whole thing. The game of "Catch the Tourist" should be an Olympic sport, 200 pounds times 25 miles per hour combine to make a mighty force. The young men said they climbed the trail three times a day, and ate rice and beans to stay in shape. I thought that the pictures of this adventure would make me the all time coolest Granny, but my grandchildren were much more interested in the picture of a big iguana sunning itself on the road.

From Monteverde we bucked and bumped our way to Tarcoles on the Pacific coast, where we had a very tame horizontal walk to see water birds in a swamp, some crocodiles in a river, some Macaws flying overhead into the setting sun, and time for us to fly home too.

Down East

Before we went on our summer trip to the east coast in 2003, we tried to do something about our wills. The financial adviser at the bank had laughed at my will because it was only two pages long, and she suggested that a "proper" will should be drawn up by a downtown lawyer that she knew. The result was a forty-page comedy of redundancy and obfuscation, all in unpronounceable legalese. My request for it to be re-written in plain language was denied. They apparently had never heard of such a thing.

I took it to a lawyer in Toronto. We called him "The Frog Prince" because he had a sort of chinless resemblance to a frog, sometimes appeared without his front tooth in place, he had rosacea, disobedient hair, rumpled clothing, and he smoked like a maniac. His office should have been condemned for all the tottering stacks of paper files on chairs, tables, desks and the floor. The carpet was stained and torn, the enormous ashtrays overflowed all over the floor, and it smelled as bad as it looked.

I liked the guy because he remembered who I was, he was always glad to see me, and sometimes he forgot to send me a bill. When he saw this 40 page will treatise, he thought it was hugely funny.

"It's computer generated at $300.00 a page", he said, and "Look here! They are making the BANK an executor! Do you know how much that will *cost*?" And then he lost my draft in his mounting tsunami of paper... Phoning lawyers offices in the phone book was useless, no secretary would set up an appointment for a will in plain language.

Mark bought a "Will Expert Family Edition" on disc, which was impossible to use because the client can never see the whole document, couldn't reconsider and go back to change anything, and it was always telling me that I had made an impossible mistake. It made me feel as though senility were creeping up on me very fast. We found a second draft of the original wills, scratched out what we didn't want, dated and signed it in front of 2 witnesses, and put done to it.

We were off to catch "The Breeze", a ferry from Toronto to Rochester, which saved us a tank of gas and about 4 hours driving. The ferry only ran the summer of 2004 and we had read in the paper that our port area wasn't very welcoming to our American friends. What an understatement! The huge slab of cement, which was the parking area, was surrounded by chain link fence, and behind that were heaps of rusted empty containers from ships, piled four high. It looked like a great habitat for the homeless, if only they had a giant can opener. We thought it might be a good place to hawk our pots, set up a lemonade and cappuccino stand, or have a taxi service to the city for the foot passengers. Anything diverting for the long wait on the hot concrete.

We were going to Cape Cod to visit Nancy Roach, who lived in a meticulous Cape Cod House in the summer, and a similarly perfect condominium in Greenwich Village in the winter. She had no messy husband, dogs, cats, children or grandchildren, and her lifestyle was a model of neatness and order. I followed Mark-the-messy-man everywhere, picking up his magazines, books, papers, packages of nuts, candy bar wrappers, jackets, sweaters, hats, to help maintain the order.

We went to Wellfleet, our favourite gallery town, full of beautiful buildings, gorgeous crafts, and handmade clothing. We had seafood for lunch on a patio with a splendid view of Cape Cod Bay over salt flats with boats and birds floating daintily on the water.

It is always fun to go to Provincetown too, but the transvestites of the world were gathering for Carnival Week with parades, dances, drag bingo, and awards, such as Most Outrageous, Mess in a Dress, and Biggest Hair. We could tell that there would be no room for us in P. town because we saw the huge line of cars going north. Later we went on a wonderful "Dune Buggy" ride. The vehicles were not actually dune buggies. They were high station wagons with the tires only half-full of air. The cars had great suspension, and it was a good thing the roof was high because we really bounced. Out on the dunes there are about 15 shacks, which have no electricity or running water. Eugene O'Neil wrote several plays while he lived in a shack. Artists, even very old ones, still like to spend time alone in the dunes. Our

236

driver told us that she had rescued Annie Dillard the writer only a week before. Ms Dillard had wandered off, and our driver made the rescue and called someone to take her home. There's a hermit who lives in the dunes full time, with a solar panel to run his computer. Only the cars for the dune rides were allowed out there, other people had to use bicycles or go on foot. To get out to the eastern beach, the cars needed an expensive license, but for 8 weeks in the summer the plovers were nesting, so people were not allowed out there. The sand shifted all the time and never got hard packed, so it's slippery to drive on. Several times our driver called ahead to see if another car was on the other side of a hill. Then she honked a few times, laughed and said, "Well here goes" as she put her foot to the floor and the car did a mighty leap to clear the hill.

At Cotuit on the south shore we saw the work of two nutty artists, the Cahouns, who painted charming pictures of mermaids smoking cigarettes with long cigarette holders, doing the laundry, making pies, holding babies, playing baseball, and flirting outrageously with human sailors. We were lucky to see this comprehensive show of the Cahoun's work because it was from many collections, and they have been dead for 40 years.

Because of Nancy's bad right knee, we usually drove in our pedestrian little Subaru, but once in a while, when Mark was busy downloading stuff on the computer, Nancy would take out her wicked cool convertible. In pristine condition, it is sparkly dark brown on the outside, leather on the inside. One day as we started off, feeling like Thelma and Louise, Mark said,

"Don't get picked up, girls!"

As soon as we got to the beach, a guy came up and stroked the flank of the car, murmuring endearments; he offered to trade his wife for Nancy's convertible. He admired every detail, asked how many cylinders it had, but Nancy had to confess that she didn't know. She could de-construct Hamlet, but anything mechanical defied her.

I always miss having had a Dad when I am sitting on a beach, and love to watch fathers interacting with their kids. One family of 2 boys and a little girl were getting pretty ratty with each other by the end of the day. The little girl had a very small dead fish that she wanted to take home. Her older brother was a pest and he kept throwing sand at it, and then french fries into her pail with the fish in it. The little girl was frantic about her fish and her mother kept saying she couldn't take it home because it would smell. Her brother continued to torture her. When Dad arrived with the car, the little girl kept saying in her tiny voice "Dad...Dad...Dad," while he was loading the car, and then when he was done, he quietly took her by the hand and they walked together to the sea so she could let the fish go back home.

At Nancy's house we checked our e-mail, Mark had 150 messages in three days, I told him he should have a separate address for his penis for all the enhancement spam he gets.

The drive up to Bar Harbor was fraught with speeding ass-biting SUVs, rain, and fog. The passage on the ferry to Yarmouth started with dramatic thunder and lightning, I was hoping my will would hold out as we sailed off into fog so dense that we couldn't even see the water. Because it was so cold, Mark was his embarrassing sartorially challenged self. On the bottom he wore his pajamas, navy blue fleece, with elastic around the ankles; they balloon out a bit. On top of that he wore two different plaid shirts and some long shorts with lots of pockets. Socks and sandals finished the bottom, and an Irish Tweed driving cap on top. At home I am used to this get-up, but it was going to cause me major embarrassment if he wore it into my brother's place. He changed behind a bush in John's driveway.

We were welcomed in Yarmouth by a live piper, which reminded me of the Englishman's remark, the first time he heard the pipes. "Thank God they don't smell!"

My brother John and his family greeted us with huge fresh lobsters for dinner. Their daughter Becca was teaching dance in Halifax, and her two-year-old son Jasper was being minded by his grandparents who are new to this game. I was prepared to dive in and be the great Domestic Goddess, having 6 grandchildren, ranging from age one to sixteen.

On Sunday we went for a drive down the coast, through Mahone Bay and Lunenburg, visited rug-hooking galleries, looked at folk art, and had a beautiful lunch by the bay full of sailboats. Dinner was at a fine new house just beyond Lunenburg, belonging to my cousin Agar Adamson and his wife Liz. The house had no furniture or rugs yet, so Jasper had a wonderful time making lots of noise to hear his echo. His father sang in the chorus at the Met when he was a boy - and Jasper will surely follow - he couldn't say very much yet, but he could sure project his voice and emotions! The Adamson's Newfoundland dog cleaned Jasper's face for him after dinner, one big lick from bottom to top.

John, the master of the snide comment, was in good form. One day, when Cath had spent about an hour trying to get Jasper to sleep, she came downstairs looking all frazzled, and said, "Whew! I sang every song I know - my full repertoire. Finally he went to sleep".

"Probably in self defense" said John.

With so much experience as a grandmother, I thought I would be a big help with Jasper but no. On a walk in town, Cath and I looked like luddite sisters trying to figure out how to collapse the stroller, and with un-grannylike cursing we gave it a good kick and stuffed it in the trunk uncollapsed. High chairs used to be simple - just a chair with a tray in front. Now there are 10 different buttons to push, a new kind of harness with three snaps. I have been aware for some time that there is a plot out there to make me think I'm getting senile, and trying to figure out the new gizmos and gadgets which one needs with a two year old seems to be another part of the plan. Moving the car seat, taking apart and cleaning the sippy cups - some of them had 5 parts - all the buttons, catches, latches, buckles and clips on kid stuff - a degree in domestic engineering is no joke anymore!

Jasper liked to play in the car, speaking of buttons. He burned out the battery by leaving the overhead light on, and locked himself in.

Cath had a cute little hand held battery driven tape recorder, about the size of half an egg, and I had the bright idea of getting Becca to record a message for Jasper. Something like,

"Hi Jasper, this is Mummy, I hope you eat your dinner and go to bed like a good boy, I love you!"

But Jasper was completely unhinged by it; he thought his mother had been put into the tiny box. He strained so hard to pull it apart I thought he would give himself hemorrhoids. He woke up at 2 in the morning screaming for his Daddy.

Just before we left, Mark and I went to a wonderful Linen shop where there was a classy yellow linen shirt. I was encouraging him to buy it, but he said "I'll have to renounce myself if I buy this shirt, and I'll need a new bank account"

Slug Goddess

Margaret Atwood wrote an article for a gardening magazine that came out in January 2004. She wrote about her shady garden, which generated a plethora of slugs. She didn't know what to do with the problem, lamenting that the shade would always generate slugs, and then she wrote that she needed a slug goddess. January is a dead time for potters, and this seemed to be a great challenge. I made a whole family of slugs. They are about a foot high, and the king and queen have gold crowns. I called Alison Gordon, who is a mutual friend, and she set up an appointment for tea with Ms. Atwood. We arrived at the appointed time, but were ushered into the garden, so we had no time to snoop at the paintings, furniture and books in the house. Madame was out buying cookies for tea, and when she arrived back, she took off her hat and dark glasses and launched into a long question period with Alison, whether she had made phone calls and arrangements for a trip to Point Pelee to watch the bird migration. In the middle of this, Alison suddenly said, "Peggy, this is Mary Lazier," and Peggy said, "I assumed that!" I left the slug goddess with her, and she sent me a post card the next day to say thank you.

I started making a lot of stoneware mermaids and mermen which loll about in party mode around a small pond which we had dug a couple of years ago. The raccoons have no respect for them and I find my poor babies with broken arms and tails. Sometimes I find

them at the bottom of the pond.

Last year Mark borrowed a live trap and he slept on the couch in the living room with the front door open, so he could hear the trap shut when it caught something. When I got up in the morning he was gone, but there was a note: 2AM gone to the dump – crossed out. 4 AM gone to the dump – crossed out. 6AM gone to the dump. He caught about 18 raccoons that way, and delivered them all to the same spot near the dump, hoping that the family could stay together. We were warned that they would return, so he sprayed a few with red paint, but we never saw them again. Potters love tools, and one of the best is a pair of Raku tongs which we keep next to the front door. These are long handled tongs for pulling red hot pots out of a kiln. They are well designed for grabbing things at a distance. Last year Mark grabbed a raccoon and wheeled him around his head a few times before he flung it off into the woods. This year they seem to be keeping their distance.

Our cat, MuMu, died June 21 2006. He was a handsome black and white tuxedo cat who was a great mouser, and so good looking that he had a fan club. On December 23 2006, our friend Theresa phoned from Global Pet Foods in Alliston to say that there was a very handsome tabby at the store and I should go over there to meet him. It was two days before Christmas though, and I was too busy. On Christmas Eve, we had Ruth and Luke and their "little sister" Natasha for dinner, when a customer arrived to buy a hanging birdbath. I knew she worked for Global Pet Foods, so I asked if she knew the cat "Cody". Well yes she did, as a matter of fact, he was in her car. She brought the cat in, opened the cage door, and he was gone in a flash, into the basement. Down there is an abomination of cobwebs, old boots, junk, off-season clothes etc. Of course everyone wanted to go down to get the cat, but he was nowhere to be found. It took days for him to emerge, all covered in cobwebs. We gave him some homeopatheic "rescue remedy" which made all the difference. Cody was a cat reared for science. I guess people who do that dislike cats, and Cody was lucky that the lab for which he was destined lost its funding before he was used. Apparently he was to have replaced a cat that became insensitive to anesthetic and had to be killed. Cody had never seen windows before, and during the spring he caught many flies and ate them. He wouldn't be picked up, but allowed some patting and tummy rubbing on the floor. I thought he would like a kitten to play with because he was raised with cats, so when we heard of a litter in March, we put our name down for an 8 week old male. This kitten entertains us 24 hours a day, and Cody is a great babysitter during the night, when we like to sleep, but during the day, Cody goes out to avoid the brat cat whose name is Spike, and whose favourite night-time activity is to investigate my hair to see if he can find a lactating supernumerary nipple. When he was still a small kitten his chin blew up like a balloon, and I took him to the vet, thinking Cody had bitten him. The vet said that he had a grub called cuterebra living in his neck. The grub had to be removed surgically, and we had to cover all entries to "under the deck" where these things are living.

It took a long time to build up a clientele in the country, but now we have 2 stores in Toronto and 6 stores in the country. In 2007, I was invited put work in a new show called "On The Table", which was held at The Gardiner Museum. The opening was in February, the night of a huge snowstorm. A lot of people didn't get to the opening because of the weather, but the show was impressive. My handmade dinner set was next to work by Robin Hopper, Harlan House, Walter Ostrom, Matthias Ostermann, and Roger Kerslake among other Canadian greats. The catalogue is 150 pages in full colour with a message on the back cover by John Ralston Saul, the husband of Adrienne Clarkson, our recent Governor General. I couldn't speak to her that night, but the following weekend we went to a Canadian-Chinese wedding in Toronto, and there she was again, so I had a rare chance to discuss my work with her.

Aaron came to visit us in the spring, driving his veggie car. He has a diesel Volkswagen car that is hooked up to a big can of used deep frying canola oil. He came all the way from PEI for about $5.00 in diesel fuel, which he needed to start up the engine. He travelled a mile or so until the engine is warm, stopped the car, and switched to the canola. His car smelled like french fries.

In April I taught a pottery class at John Ross Robertson Public School, where my twin grandsons attended the kindergarten. The night before, I stayed overnight at their house, and after dinner, I told the boys that I lived on their street when I was a little girl, and I went to their school.

"My picture is in the front hall, I'll take you to see it tomorrow before class", said I, thinking of my graduation picture, in which my head was less than a centimetre high. A silence ensued, and then, wide-eyed, Charlie said,

"Granny Green-car, are you Queen Elizabeth?"

Some of Mary's pottery may be seen at *www.redhen.ca*

Some shops that carry Mary's work:

Gardiner Museum of Ceramic Art, Toronto

Fawn Ceramics, Distillery district, Toronto

Drift, Cookstown, Ontario

Dragonfly, Orangeville, Ontario

Dufferin County Museum and Archives

Burdette Gallery, Marsville, Ontario